Parental Alienation 911 Workbook

By

Jill Egizii

&

Judge Michele Lowrance

> *The best thing that can happen is that your children re-connect with you. The worst thing that can happen is that you never try.*

Introductions

Waste Not A Moment

By Jill Egizii

I come to you, the alienated parent with a different perspective than my friend, Judge Michele. She shares very important, even priceless tools that have never been offered by any member of the legal community. I am one of you. I am an alienated parent and I will share my insights and practical thoughts on how to cope with the loneliness, heart break and sadness that accompany parental alienation. This workbook will give you the skills and tools that you need to wait actively for your children to come home. I hope that it will take you from existing to living again. I hope that it will allow you to become a strong voice for you and for your children. You can become an effective advocate who creates awareness and educates the public and professional community about the risks, results and remedies of and for parental alienation.

You may still be wondering if what you are experiencing is in fact parental alienation, or if as in my case, you have already spent years outside your children's lives, then this workbook will answer most of your questions. We will give you many valuable tips that will allow you to become stronger, wiser, and steadfast in your journey to make sense of your current situation.

We will help you identify alienation from its inception and so you can gauge how severe your parental alienation has become. This enables you to take a proactive role in stopping or reversing the damage done to the once loving relationship that you shared with your child.

They say that hindsight is 20/20. If I only had this workbook and the truths I now know about parental alienation 8 years ago. I believe that I would have handled my situation much differently. At the time I didn't know where to turn. I didn't know how to respond, think, or even feel. This book is a primer for anyone new to the idea of parental alienation or for those that have experienced it for years without sufficient answers. It is a collection of what I wish I would have known...then. This is what we have learned from the tens of thousands of individual heart breaking stories that I have collected over the years.

My horoscope on Christmas Eve said it all. It is the mantra that I live by each and every day. "There is no use wondering if everything will work out. It already has. There is no other time and place than right now". While this may be difficult for some alienated parents to digest, the philosophy is one that Judge Michele and I preach constantly. Live your life. Don't live for what is missing, but for what you have right now. Remember to always ask yourself, "Who do you want to be when your children grow up?"

My Best to you,

Jill Egizii

Parental Alienation - A Corrosive Legacy

By Judge Michele Lowrance

I have been a judge on the divorce bench for 16 years and have watched the corrosive legacy of parental alienation and visitation interference play out over decades. We have no statistics for measuring this group because the victims are too vast. But the concentric circles include the children, their children, and the extended family as well. The declaration of war by one parent on another creates radioactive fallout which contaminates for generations.

The alienating parent treats the target parent like a disease in the child that must be removed. They make the child's survival contingent upon such removal. So the child must extricate the target parent without the privilege of grieving the loss. These are crippling circumstances.

I have witnessed impassioned declarations of love for a child by an alienating parent to masquerade the venom he/she feels for the other parent. Parents who do this are not interested in mere control. Their stakes are higher: total annihilation of the target parent's bond with the child. Little by little, alienation in a divorce case starts to take root. And when it fully takes root, I see the child's boundaries collapse before my eyes. Soon the child forgets how to protect him or herself, and must align with the alienating parent as if life depends on it -- because it does.

In the future perhaps this degenerating influence maybe addressed by therapy. But for now, we can and must do better. I want to tell you how to be proactive in court and how to fight against the inclination to give up like so many hurt, alienated parents -- who are, frankly, not always welcomed in the courts.

Here are some reasons why judges often have no love for these difficult cases:

Professional or litigants who don't really understand the full definition and qualities of Parental Alienation often misuse the concept in the court. Often professionals or litigants don't differentiate between, for example, oppositional disorder, anxiety disorder or even transitional anger at the parent versus parental alienation. Judges also often think that a parent may be claiming parental alienation because they don't want to take responsibility for the breakdown of the parent child relationship.

Combative parents present conflicting "he said/she said" stories making it very difficult to determine who is telling the truth. Often an alienating parent comes to believe what he or she is saying and their presentation seems authentic.

When targeted parents present their side of the case, they are often angry and frustrated -- they often seem defensive even when they are telling the truth. As a result, they don't present very well in court. Judges often consider attitude as influential as content.

The children often support the alienating parent by telling the judge, their attorney, and mental health professionals how they have been treated badly, and of their dislike for the target parent. Programmed children lose their critical reasoning skills and their ability to choose freely.

Alienated children often won't cooperate with therapeutic intervention and courts have difficulty enforcing these orders.

Judges like to believe that what they do works and is the right decision. When their decisions don't work, they often get exasperated with both parties.

Extended family and friends who love the child and would provide a nurturing and healthy family life are eliminated. Once the cutting out of a parent has occurred the child is left under the full care of perhaps a very dysfunctional parent.

Alienating parents can have personality disorders, high energy, and the ability to be creative about manipulation of court orders. They often represent themselves even in appeals and complaints to professional bodies.

Because mediation and therapeutic interventions are not effective enough, especially in severe cases, targeted parents must rely on the courts to help them have access to their children. Unfortunately few people, including judges, attorneys, and therapists understand the COMPLEX nature of the problem.

Despite these difficulties there is plenty that you can do. Jill and I have devoted this workbook to tell you what we have learned from our two different perspectives. This includes the emotional and legal aspects. This workbook is not meant to be a compendium of legal studies or psychological research. We will direct you to that in our bibliography and reading suggestions.

This workbook is to help you process your own experience so that you can escalate your brain into problem solving mode. You may be among the many alienated parents I have known, who have grown weary due to the repetitive stress fracture on your heart. Each time your visitation is interfered with, it has a cumulative effect. This can make you hyper sensitive, which easily magnifies your emotional response. When you react with hatred, you not only play into their hands, you're letting them steer your ship, letting them determine your present and future. It is our hope that you will benefit from the tools we've organized. We spend a good amount of time on ways to control your anger, which you already know can be a built in enemy.

If your reactions are based upon what has been done to you, you can only respond with hatred. When you do this, you give the alienating parent the "upper hand," because he or she has provoked you to become the hateful person who they are portraying you to be to the children. We want to help you not let someone else provoke, influence, and therefore control how you behave. You run the risk of actually becoming as miserable and dysfunctional of a person as they're trying to portray you to your children.

It is my hope and intention to help you not to get caught in the cycle that I see play out all the time in court. When you are caught in the cycle you will become worn out and lose your stamina. When you react in anger you lose your ability to create a strategy or be solution oriented. This is part of what wears you out and keeps you locked into catastrophic thinking.

The tools in this book are geared to keep you from escalating and giving up. When you act in response to emotions it is equivalent to a 911 call, which really should be a 411 call. (Get information). This is the aim of the workbook.

As you read this, you may be on the edge of giving up. You may be starting to feel that nothing can work against your former spouse's devotion to destroy your relationship with your children. There may be situations that you may believe are unalterable like the alienating parent suffering from narcissism, borderline disorder, or sociopath but that still does not give you license to further destroy yourself.

Even though you may be physically invisible to your children, you will always be visible to them through stories, gossip, and second hand reporting from all sources. When we lose a loved one, we often decide to live the way that the departed person would have wanted us to. In the same spirit, when you lose a child to alienation, you need to live as if he or she is watching you. We want to help you reach your long term goal; to become the person your child wants to come home to.

Contents

Table of Contents

Manifest *Your* Future

Developing A 'Manifesto'

The writing of a Manifesto I have been told regularly is one of the most valuable parts of my (Judge Michele) book *The Good Karma Divorce.* For people enduring parental alienation or severe visitation interference it is most vital. A life crisis pushes one to choose a new path. At first it's easy to allow yourself to vent your pain, to behave any way you feel like. The process of developing a personal manifesto puts you in a position to consciously choose your path through this darkness.

When it comes to divorce and custody battles there are unfortunately no pain-free, quick fixes. Because of this I started developing techniques to use in my courtroom aimed at reducing pain and turmoil in complicated child-custody cases.

Step One of this process is to have each person write down their *worst fears* about their relationship with their children, about the other party's parenting and their goals for the future of these relationships. It became clear that the simple act of writing these fears down offered opportunities for emotional breakthroughs. Often hidden fears create the kind of emotional blocks that prevent resolution. I saw for

1

myself how having people write things down made a tangible difference in the outcomes. Your Personal Manifesto may include any or all of the following:

- How you feel

- Reactive behaviors you want to change

- How those changes will benefit your life

- The kind of person you would like to be

- Acknowledgment of your progress

- Your intentions for your future

Neuroscientists have demonstrated that writing engages the part of the brain that activates problem-solving and analyzing while *de*activating the part of the brain where emotions (like fear and anger) are generated. When you take the time to 'label' what you're feeling with words (i.e. write) this forces the emotional part of your mind to 'hit the brakes' so you can enter problem-solving mode.

Writing is one way to put your pain to work *for* you. When you dump your emotions on the page, you free up emotional energy you can now apply to other things...like managing your feelings.

Physicians, sociologists, theologians, psychologists, and philosophers all agree that the death of a mate or child is one of life's greatest stressors. While alienation is not 'death'; for many target parents alienation is an emotional equivalent, separation.

This Manifesto process is designed to become your map toward becoming the person you *want* to be on the other side of this crisis. Developing a manifesto sheds enough light on the situation that you can begin to see the positive potential your future holds.

A Manifesto, or mission statement is; an organizing principle that will serve as your emotional beacon during the dark times. Your Manifesto will help you focus on your goals and aspirations for yourself and your family. This will be essential especially during times when you are in so much pain you can't focus on your goals and aspirations for yourself and your children.

The Manifesto process is individual. There are no rules, just a few guidelines to get you started. Your Personal Manifesto may be half a page long or a dozen. You may find yourself writing down things you've never told *any*one — so keep this in a safe place so you can be brutally, blazingly honest, and completely unselfconscious. Grammar doesn't matter. Neither does spelling or penmanship. No one should ever see these but you.

That being said — a side note about what is 'discoverable' in a divorce action. Anything you write *could* be subpoenaed if it is determined to be relevant. This includes your diary, a letter to your sister, even your emails. These writings are discoverable so if your attorney asks you to write these things down it can be considered work product. Even if this document is found it shows your aspiration to be the best parent you can be.   If it says negative things about yourself and your parenting, write it, learn from it, and throw it out.

Don't worry about perfection while creating your Manifesto. Striving for perfection is the enemy of getting things done, particularly work of this emotional nature.

The Manifesto process encourages you to note the good and the bad in your experiences with your children. These notes may remind you of *good* memories and help you recognize that you don't have to corrupt all your good memories in order to detach from the pain you are trying to manage. The Manifesto process helps you investigate a more balanced picture of your story.   As you think through the following warm-up questions, write your answers, make notes include any insights that emerge.

Here are a series of questions designed to get you thinking.

Write five things about your children that you treasure. Note these with as much emotional detail and examples as possible.

_____
_____
_____
_____
_____
_____
_____
_____
_____
_____
_____
_____
_____
_____
_____
_____
_____
_____
_____
_____

Write down five hurts your children (and/or spouse using your children) have inflicted upon you. Note how you reacted. Most important to the process...note how your reaction did or didn't pay off; what were the consequences of your reaction?

_____
_____
_____
_____
_____
_____
_____
_____
_____
_____
_____
_____
_____
_____
_____

Picture and describe the kind of parent you **want** to be now. How would you like to behave, be perceived now today? How do you want to be perceived five years from now about what you were like during this hard time? How do you want your children perceive your current behavior five years from now?

_____
_____
_____
_____
_____
_____
_____
_____
_____
_____
_____
_____

List all the positive qualities you think a good parent should have. Next to each put a plus sign if you think you have that quality and a minus sign if you think that needs improvement.

_____
_____
_____
_____
_____
_____
_____
_____
_____
_____
_____
_____
_____

Describe the ideal way you'd like to be able to handle your disappointment and resentment. If you were the best version of you...how would you handle it all?

_____
_____
_____
_____
_____
_____
_____
_____
_____
_____
_____
_____
_____

Make a list of things you are waiting for, things you want to have happen in your life before you can believe it is "good". Next to each item, note whether you believe that your alienation situation is keeping you from that.

_____
_____
_____
_____
_____
_____
_____
_____
_____
_____
_____
_____

Write your doubts that you will be able to find peace and resolution from this situation.

_____
_____
_____
_____
_____
_____
_____
_____
_____
_____
_____
_____
_____
_____

Now let's reframe those negatives through 're-writing'. Take each fear or negative listed above and rephrase it in a way that puts you back in control. For example if you wrote..."I worry all the time". You'd convert that into a positive by writing "I think things through and consider my choices carefully". If anger is a dominant factor in your emotional state, you might write "I want to express my feelings without hurting anyone".

_____
_____
_____
_____
_____
_____
_____
_____
_____
_____
_____
_____
_____

Don't be surprised if your Manifesto develops in stages. You won't have perfectly polished document but you *will* dump the poisons on the page so you can think straight. Plus, you'll have the beginnings of an important message to yourself.

I know it's difficult to think about creating something like the Manifesto when you don't know what will happen with your relationship with your children. But a Manifesto is vital because it creates a path that can lead to more peace and happiness. Ultimately finding peace in the midst of an alienation situation shouldn't hinge solely on the behavior of others. You can't sentence yourself to a lifetime of waiting. You can start sculpting that strong, powerful person you really want to be…right now.

Ralph Waldo Emerson said, "Sow a thought, and you reap an action; sow an action, and you reap a habit; sow a habit, and you reap a character; sow a character, and you reap a destiny". The character you described becoming in your Manifesto can influence everyone you come into contact with, for the better.

On some days your Manifesto will outshine you. It's OK if you don't fully attain your goals. Let your manifesto be your inspiration not the measuring stick you use to beat yourself up if you fall short. What matters is keeping your eye on the target.

Take all the thoughts from above and create a Manifesto with clear positive statements about what you want, how you will achieve that, and how you'll feel when these things start to happen.

Manifesto

The 20 Issues of PA

Know What Stage Of Alienation You're Experiencing

The way alienation develops is often murky and confusing. It may have taken you months or weeks to even 'figure out' that you may be experiencing the phenomenon referred to as 'alienation' from your child or children. Most people struggle to make sense of what's happening as their relationships with their children seem to be falling apart in their hands.

In fact, sometimes it seems like the more they 'try' the worse things spiral out of their control. Realizing and identifying what's actually happening is challenge number one. This exercise is aimed at putting 'where you are' in your personal situation in perspective. To help you get a grasp on the elusive nature of alienation we'll be looking at the original criteria Psychiatrist Richard A. Gardner used to describe what he called 'Parental Alienation Syndrome' as a potential psychological condition.

For now you want to become clear and open eyed about what *is actually happening* in your world, in your experience. This is the way to learn how to devise the best possible responses, the best possible choices, actions, and attitudes for healing, overcoming, or minimizing the damage alienation does to you *and* your children.

This exercise will help you identify where your situation is on the continuum from 'mild' to 'severe'. Accomplishing just this will help you feel more 'sane' and less alone. Realize that in order for all these symptoms and issues to be categorized and identified they had to happen to a large number of other people as well. This exercise will help you determine where you are now. Just accomplishing this will empower you to be able to make decisions with clarity and effectiveness based on reality and fact not based on you fears or projections. Begin by clarifying the symptoms of your parental alienation experience.

> *It is only when we have the courage to face things exactly as they are without any self-deception of illusion that a light will develop out of events by which the path to success may be recognized.*
>
> *~I Ching*

Alienation is: the systematic deterioration of one parent's relationship with their children. The purpose of alienation is for one parent (often the custodial parent) to eliminate the involvement of the parent targeted for alienation in the children's lives. Essentially children are becoming convinced to view the target parent as an aggressor, as "trying to take" the children from or interfere with the child-alienator relationship. In severe situations children may be 'programmed' by one parent to perceive the target parent as an abuser. In the worst cases children can be convinced (by the alienator) to believe in abuse or neglect by the target parent that simply did not happen.

According to experts when a child is a victim of, or unwitting accomplice to one parent's attempts at alienating the other they exhibit similar behaviors. Mild cases might exhibit only a few behaviors. The specific ingredient underlying all these traits or behaviors is programming by one parent intent on alienating the other. When mild situations grow to include more and more of these behaviors and attitudes they evolve into moderate or even severe situations. We'll begin with some characteristic behaviors and attitudes.

These exercises are designed to help you gain insight into your own behavior and also to keep a chronology of events as they developed for your attorney, the court, your therapist, or your family therapist.

Dr. William Bernet of Vanderbilt University describes the three stages of Parental Alienation as follows:

> "Yellow – Parental alienation disorder may be mild, moderate, or severe. When
> the parental alienation disorder is mild, the child may briefly resist contact
> with the alienated parent, but does have contact and enjoys a good relationship

with the alienated parent once they are together. When the parental alienation disorder is mild, the child may have a strong, healthy relationship with both parents, even though the child recites criticisms of the alienated parent.

Orange – When the parental alienation disorder is moderate, the child may persistently resist contact with the alienated parent and will continue to complain and criticize the alienated parent during the contact. The child is likely to have a mildly to moderately pathological relationship with the preferred parent.

Red – When the parental alienation disorder is severe, the child strongly and persistently resists contact and may hide or run away to avoid seeing the alienated parent. The child's behavior is driven by a firmly held, false belief that the alienated parent is evil, dangerous or worthless. The child is likely to have a strong, severely pathological relationship with the preferred parent, perhaps sharing a paranoid worldview."

Mild –Yellow

At this stage 82% of children expressed affection toward the target parent. At this level 95% of parents had their appointed parenting time.[1]

---

[1] Janelle Burrill, Parental Alienation Syndrome in Court Referred Custody Cases, Oct., 2002; Universal-Publishers. This dissertation summarizes research from court referred cases to determine the presence or absence of Parental Alienation Syndrome. The data appears to corroborate the definitions of Parental Alienation Syndrome.

ISSUE #1

The child believes he has choice about visitation.

An alienating parent may lead children to believe they have a choice as to when or whether they visit the other parent when in fact an agreement has already determined the visitation schedule. This false expectation can set the child-parent relationship for conflict. Giving children choices where they actually have no choice sets the target parent up as an intruder 'interrupting' their children's lives or 'upsetting' their schedules. Regardless of what happens the parent is now an outsider; either of not seeing his or her children at the appointed times or having to deal with angry, resentful children.

Describe any such situations you've experienced in specific detail. Where were you? What season was it? What words did your child/children use to let you know your visitation rights and times were 'infringing' in *their* lives? How or where did they get the incorrect belief that set visits were optional or 'open for discussion'? What let you know this? What words did they use? Also, record what you said or did and what you wish you had done differently.

_____
_____
_____
_____
_____
_____
_____
_____
_____
_____
_____
_____
_____
_____
_____

ISSUE #2

Child is not 'allowed' to or interested in transporting personal belongings to the target parent's residence.

An alienating parent may lead children to believe the target parent's home is not 'their' home, or is only 'temporary' and therefore undeserving of bothering with making it 'homey' for the children. This can result in a child not perceiving the non-residential parent's life, home, and environment as a true 'home' for the child. This reinforces suggestions setting the alienated parent up as an outsider 'interrupting' their children's lives or 'upsetting' their schedules and dragging them 'away from' their 'real' homes. Time with the target parent is set up as not a 'real' relationship.

Describe any such situations you've experienced in specific detail. Where were you? What season was it? What words did your children use to let you know they didn't feel your home, your life is also theirs? How did they get this idea? Also, record what you said or did and what you wish you had done differently.

_____
_____
_____
_____
_____
_____
_____
_____
_____
_____
_____
_____
_____
_____

ISSUE #3

Children being 'overscheduled' or being offered 'irresistible temptations' designed to interfere with the target parent's visitation.

When there is absolutely no flexibility in the visitation schedule to respond to the child's needs this can be an indicator of a problem growing. In some cases an alienating parent may intentionally schedule the children in so many activities that the target is essentially demoted to 'chauffer'. This means little quality time to visit. It can be difficult for the target parent to protest without appearing to be 'selfish'. Another subtle method of dissuading a child from their scheduled visitation is if the alienator parent sets up 'irresistible temptations' designed to interfere with the target parent's visitation.

In what ways has this kind of activity interfered with your visitation? How much of your time with your children is wasted driving them from activity to activity? Have any of your visits been cancelled for the child to participate in some 'irresistible' opportunity that could easily have been offered another time or day? Note them in specific detail. When were you informed of the cancellation? What words did the child use to describe 'why'? Is there a reason the co-parent couldn't have made this offer for time or day that did not conflict with visitation? Note also what the other parent's version of the story would be.

_____
_____
_____
_____
_____
_____
_____
_____
_____
_____
_____
_____

ISSUE #4

Barring the target parent's access to children's school or medical records, or their schedules or extra-curricular activities.

Like the above, these kinds of impediments in effect bar the target parent from full participation in the child's life. In what ways has this kind of block showed up in your experience?

_____

_____

_____

_____

_____

_____

_____

_____

_____

_____

_____

_____

_____

_____

_____

_____

ISSUE #5

Children become upset or sustain on-going anger toward target parent without apparent reason; offering vague or no details.

There is regular run of the mill, getting annoyed with a parent for saying no or engaging necessary discipline. This is something beyond the average day to day ups and downs of healthy parent-child relationships. Children are eager to want to be forgiven and therefore are eager to forgive if given half the chance. If 'normal' anger is reactivated, not allowed to heal, it may signal growing parental alienation. Contributing to this would be if the children claim they can't remember **any** happy times or pleasant occasions with you or if they can't name any of your positive qualities.

Recall any specific incidents of on-going low grade anger or simmering resentment the child has expressed toward you. What words or actions did the children use specifically to express this? Re-examine what went on before to be sure there wasn't some slight or conflict you may have overlooked? Has this been on-going? For how long? Has the expression of negative feelings escalated? How have you responded to them?

_____

_____

_____

_____

_____

_____

_____

_____

_____

_____

_____

_____

_____

_____

Does your child remember any good times? Claimed some happy time or event never happened? Has some event become distorted i.e. missing the positives, lacking the ups and only recalling the downs? Do you reminisce with them about happy times?

_____

_____

_____

_____

_____

_____

_____

_____

_____

_____

_____

How did you respond? Did you react? Did the reaction create a conflict?

_____
_____
_____
_____
_____
_____
_____
_____
_____
_____
_____
_____
_____

ISSUE #6

Unerring support and defense of the alienating parent.

This means that...no matter *what* the situation the child supports or defends the alienating parent. The alienating parent is right in every situation. The alienating parent's view and directions become 'facts'.

Detail any of this kind of slant in your relationship with your child. What 'facts' did your child assert and irrationally defend? Have any new or 'arbitrary' rules have been made. Ex: "I can't talk on the phone on Wednesday nights now so I can't talk to you after the game."

_____
_____
_____
_____
_____
_____
_____
_____
_____
_____
_____
_____

Have there been any conflicts from a 'tiff' to an all-out argument between parents that the children have a 'taken' on? Have they offered opinions about you being wrong and the other parent being 'right'?

_____
_____
_____
_____
_____
_____
_____
_____
_____
_____
_____
_____

Moderate – Orange

At this stage 59% of children expressed anger toward target parent. Despite this 65% of children also expressed affection for target parent. Parents had 65% of their appointed parenting time with the children.[2]

The most difficult problem with parental alienation as a whole is that the lines are blurry. Where does something *mild* become *moderate*? It's difficult to tell, hard to know. In the end all such delineations are to some degree arbitrary.

This somewhat self-defined 'line' between mild and moderate hinges on a shift from passive to 'active'. In the earlier issues the child is more or less passive. They may have defended the other parent, wittingly or unwittingly taken sides, or expressed seemingly unfounded anger, resentment, mistrust in the early issues. Because alienation is so hard to make sense of entering the moderate category is sort of like entering the twilight zone. This is when many alienated parents start to realize that there is something is seriously wrong. It's here that hindsight starts to bring the earlier issues noted above into focus.

What we may once have shrugged off as moodiness, external pressure (from the other parent) now snaps into sharp distinction when we enter the realm of

---

[2] Janelle Burrill, Parental Alienation Syndrome in Court Referred Custody Cases, Oct., 2002; Universal-Publishers. This dissertation summarizes research from court referred cases to determine the presence or absence of Parental Alienation Syndrome. The data appears to corroborate the definitions of Parental Alienation Syndrome.

moderate alienation. In these more moderate examples of alienating experiences the child begins taking an active role as you will see.

ISSUE # 7

The children have created public scenes using inappropriate language or violence to embarrass, humiliate, or denigrate the target parent.

Parents know instinctively what I mean when I say a 'scene'. It should be clear how such behaviors indicate alienation might be happening. If such incidents have happened in your relationships describe them in detail. Did the offending event put an end to a visitation? What do you do about this 'scene'? Was it helpful?

_____
_____
_____
_____
_____
_____
_____
_____
_____
_____
_____
_____
_____
_____

Even if an actual altercation or disagreement started 'naturally' alienation trained children will exploit any potential opportunity for conflict (no matter how small) into a humiliating unpleasant scene for the parent. Have any genuine altercations escalated irrationally? If so describe the initial conflict and record the escalation. Are there reoccurring themes that start conflict? Are there things you do that seem to start conflict?

_____
_____
_____
_____
_____
_____
_____
_____
_____
_____
_____
_____
_____
_____

ISSUE #8

The child is physically or psychologically "rescued" from a visit with the target parent.

Rescue can mean the child uses the 'cell phone' as a weapon to bring the 'other parent' into the mix. If they can't get their way, if they have to go somewhere they'd rather not, eat something they'd rather not and call the other parent in to interfere this is 'rescue'. Of course telephone interference is the thin edge of the wedge. At its more extreme the other parent swoops in to 'physically rescue' the child. The alienator parent arrives on the scene during the target parent's visit and literally 'saves' the child from some *perceived* danger. It may be something as small as the target parent is 'making' the child attend their cousin's dance recital, the child calls the other parent claiming anything from not feeling well ('and target parent won't take me home')... to false accusations of verbal or physical abuse.

We can see how the behaviors become more clearly antagonistic, more distinctly alienating as they evolve. Here we begin to see how earlier issues such as making visits and communication with the target parent 'optional' conspire to create ripe grounds for this escalated level of behaviors.

The key here is that when the alienating parent goes around 'rescuing' the children when there is *no threat to their safety*, they establish and reinforce the idea that the target parent is either inept or an outright danger. Both such scenarios serve the ultimate purpose of undermining the child sense of the target parent's reliability and safe-ness.

Describe any such situations that you've experienced in detail. How did it start? How did the 'rescue' transpire? What 'excuses' were given for why the child had to leave/ be taken home to settle down, etc.?

If you are using these incidents for court make sure you keep a record of the dates these events happened and any witnesses or emails.

_____
_____
_____
_____
_____
_____
_____
_____
_____
_____
_____
_____

What was the end result? Did you lose the rest of that visit? How much of a visit did you lose?

_____

_____

_____

_____

_____

_____

_____

_____

_____

_____

_____

_____

_____

How did you feel?   Did you recognize the dynamic?   Did you 'get' what was

happening? Were you secretly relieved when 'help' arrived? It can be hard to admit

that our children's behavior can scare us. It's hard to know how to handle a child's

melt down for even the most loving and confident parent. But when you're a parent

who is already facing marginalization and attacks on your ability this kind of

behavior can stupefy you. It's beyond difficult to know how to respond. Perhaps in

retrospect is it possible your reaction escalated the problem?

_____
_____
_____
_____
_____
_____
_____
_____
_____
_____
_____
_____
_____

Understand that in such situations there is no 'right thing to do'. You are being set up (intentionally or accidentally) for failure. For future reference the only thing to do is to remain **as calm as possible**. Say and do as little as possible. Offer only comfort and sympathy. Don't attack the 'rescuer' *even if* you are right and they are wrong. If possible, offer reasonable alternatives to them sweeping off with the children. "If he's not feeling well I could run by the clinic and then bring him home as scheduled..."

In hindsight, is there a way you might have minimized this situation? What can you do if there's a next time, to recognize when this may be 'brewing' in the child/children? What signs, indicators, and behaviors did they exhibit that hinted that an explosion was coming? What might you say or do to deflect or diminish something like this before it 'explodes'?

_____
_____
_____
_____
_____
_____
_____
_____
_____
_____
_____
_____
_____
_____
_____

ISSUE # 9

The children disregard the target parent's feelings; express NO apparent guilt about conspiring against the target parent.

Perhaps what is most shocking and painful about this issue is the child's total absence of guilt over cruelty to or exploitation of the alienated parent. They have been taught that the target parent is the 'enemy'. Financial or 'gift' exploitation is a 'justifiable' behavior according to the alienating parent because of the financial problems the divorce caused or because child support is 'not enough'.

it this level, the child shows no ambivalence about their animosity toward the target parent. Again it's hard to know where to 'draw the line' between mild, moderate, and severe. But this issue describes a state of belief in which the target parent is routinely denigrated, is treated with cruelty from the child, or is perhaps even out and out exploited, bribed, manipulated into buying things or doing favors with the promise that the child will 'behave', be nice, and participate in their scheduled visits or phone calls.

In other words a savvy child begins to manipulate the parent's emotions, the parent's desire to 'be' with the child for personal gain. And again, to some degree all children learn (and try to master) this skill. The difference is *these* children have the support (and often coaching) of the other parent.

Be clear about an instance where your child knowingly and willfully said or did things designed to hurt you without demonstrating any genuine remorse. Note the details of the experience. Sure every child will pull out the occasional 'I hate you', but most children will apologize in some way. That is when the hurts were said 'accidentally' in the heat of the moment or in the fullness of emotion. At this level of alienation, a child can shout hurtful things at the target and exhibit triumph and did not display any remorse or concern.

Log any such experiences as you've experienced them.

ISSUE # 10

The target parent has lost parenting time with the child.

No matter what the cause, no matter what the excuse...when you get down to the nitty-gritty, the child is not or has not been spending the scheduled time with the targeted parent. It could be a series of thin excuses, 'doctor appointments, dental appointments, friend's parties, extra-curricular activities', the list is endless of ways for an enterprising parent or child to find to keep the target parent out of their day to day life.

Recently in a small town outside Springfield, IL a father was shot to death by his ex-mother-in-law while attempting to pick up his alienated child for their court appointed visit. This is obviously the most extreme example of someone, in this case the grandmother, blocking visitation. In most states visitation interference is illegal...as illegal as failure to pay child support. However, unlike unpaid child support, this visitation interference (unfortunately) is too often considered a very low level offense and the complaint is often added to the 'growing file'. You should log each time this happens.

For now log every specific event of missed visitation or cancelled phone calls or any of the ways you've been kept from your appointed times. Note them in as much detail as possible. Go back in time to see if there has been a pattern of such behavior. What may have seemed innocent schedule conflicts months ago may begin to reveal a pattern you hadn't yet detected. This also will be included in your mapping the history of the alienation.

_____
_____
_____
_____
_____
_____
_____
_____
_____
_____
_____
_____
_____

Since interrupted or blocked visitation is one of the few tangibles you can demonstrate to the court you should keep a careful log of such things as they happen. Use this information as a useful, clear presentation to a family court judge. That's why it's important to be detailed and accurate now while devising your list.

_____
_____
_____
_____
_____
_____
_____
_____
_____
_____
_____
_____
_____
_____

ISSUE # 11

The child demonstrates fear or hatred of the target parent.

This is when the children claim to be 'harassed', frightened, or upset by the target parent's attempts to make contact with them, even for required visits or phone calls. If the child is suddenly 'afraid' of being alone with, or driving in the car with, or going to the residence of the target parent this is severe.

If when you try to meet your child at the appointed times there is a last minute 'schedule' change or the child has an emotional outburst that cancels your visit, you may have entered the realm of your child demonstrating fear or hatred. At this stage some of your visits may work, others may blow up in your face. At this stage you still see and engage with your child even if some attempts are fruitless and end in tears (yours or theirs).

The underlying issue here is the child has attached negative feelings to the target parent that are so strong that their 'feelings' become the visitation and relationship obstacle more so than any outside pressures. Psychiatrists and psychologists will point out that at this point the external pressure from the alienating parent has internalized.

The child *believes* the negative beliefs about the target parent are their own organic thoughts and feelings. This level demonstrates that the child has internalized all the negatives about the target parent that have been floating around their lives. They collect them from the alienating parent, from that parent's conversations (complaints) about the target parent with other family member or friends and have officially adopted such thinking for themselves.

Describe any such experiences you've undergone in your child/parent relationship. As usual, be detailed. Describe what happened, describe how the event transpired.

_____
_____
_____
_____
_____
_____
_____
_____
_____
_____
_____
_____
_____
_____

ISSUE # 13

The child 'spies' or covertly gathers information for the alienating parent to use against the target parent.

This may be an extension of the 'smear' campaign as this might be how the alienating parent and child find the personal 'ammo' they needed to further upset, interfere with, the target parent's relationship with the child; while justifying their position. It also serves the function of keeping the animosity fresh by continually gaining new material to keep resentment alive.

This 'tactic' assumes that the child is still participating in visits with the target parent at least superficially. The child at this point does not threaten to 'not go' with the target parent. The child seemingly behaves normally but eavesdrops on conversations at the check-out register, if the target parent speaks to friends within earshot of the child the child will 'know' everything. The child may even be prompted to peek at the target parent's checkbook or QuickBooks or even in extreme cases; steal.

Have you discovered your children sneaking, eavesdropping or otherwise spying on you? Has any oddly personal or confidential information 'ended up' in the hands of your ex-spouse who then used the information against you? There are a thousand ways this might happen. Junior brings back to Mom the price of Daddy's new fiancée's engagement ring. Sally reports to daddy that Mom has a new credit card. Any such transfer of confidential or personal information is an example. Note any such experiences you've had in as much detail as possible.

_____
_____
_____
_____
_____
_____
_____
_____
_____
_____
_____
_____

Note if you reacted. If the ex came at you accusing of 'skimming child support to pay for the ring'...how did you react? Also note the consequences of your 'reaction': did the 'fight' escalate? Did you engage the fight or 'walk away'? What else might you try next time?

ISSUE # 14

The child resists or opposes meaningful contact or insists on spending less time with the target parent.

At this point in the parental alienation situation the child herself starts bucking visitation. While earlier issues of lost visitation may have been in the power of the alienating parent, at this stage the child willingly participates in sabotaging the target parent's visits. At this stage the child seemingly has all the 'power' in the parent/child relationship.

On the more benign end of the spectrum the child may claim they are busy or have other plans and only avoid some visits. Further along the spectrum, the child may be throwing tantrums or otherwise intentionally humiliating the target parent whenever they are together. At this stage the child has taken over denying the target parent time and visits from the alienating parent. At this stage if a child is 'forced' to choose, they will almost certainly choose the alienating parent.

Has your child/children ever been the one to refuse to participate in visits? Explain how the event(s) transpired in as much detail as possible.

_____
_____
_____
_____
_____
_____
_____
_____
_____
_____
_____
_____
_____

How did you respond to the situation? Did your approach solve or exacerbate the situation? How might you better respond if this happens again?

_____
_____
_____
_____
_____
_____
_____
_____
_____
_____
_____
_____
_____

Severe—Red

At this stage 90% of children expressed *anger* toward the target parent. Despite this 45% of the children **also expressed affection** for the target parent. In addition 60% of the children had joined in the denigration of the target parent. Only 15% of children had 'visitation' time with target parent.[3]

---

[3] Janelle Burrill, Parental Alienation Syndrome in Court Referred Custody Cases, Oct., 2002; Universal-Publishers. This dissertation summarizes research from court referred cases to determine the presence or absence of Parental Alienation Syndrome. The data appears to corroborate the definitions of Parental Alienation Syndrome.

Again one of the most difficult problems with parental alienation as a whole is that the lines are blurry. Where does something moderate become severe? It's difficult to tell, hard to know. In the end such delineations are to some degree arbitrary.

This 'line' between moderate and severe hinges on a shift from 'active' to 'aggressive'. In the moderate issues the child is active. They defend the other parent, take sides, or express seemingly unfounded anger, resentment, mistrust. It's in the moderate category when many alienated parents start to realize that something is seriously wrong. At the severe level things deteriorate much more extremely.

What had been passive, then active, becomes outright aggression as you will see.

ISSUE # 15

The child has declared that he/she does not want to see or have further contact with the target parent.

It doesn't matter what form the 'message' comes in; voice mail, text, e-mail, snail mail, a Facebook wall post...the possibilities are endless. The issue here is the child himself asserts that they do not want to have any kind of relationship with the target parent.

Has your child/children sent you this message? How did it transpire? Include as much detail as possible.

_____
_____
_____
_____
_____
_____
_____
_____
_____
_____
_____
_____

How did you react? What effect did your reaction have?

_____
_____
_____
_____
_____
_____
_____
_____
_____
_____
_____
_____

ISSUE #16

The alienating parent initiates a scenario forcing the child to choose between one parent and the other.

This may include any suggestions for change of residence or inquiries about changing the child's name or suggesting that a stepparent adopt the child. This may include attempts to or actually moving to an inconvenient location for the target parent to visit. Essentially this issue means someone is asking the child to abandon the target parent. Of course asking the child to choose one parent over the other causes severe distress.

This may mean forcing the child to make such a declaration for family court or perhaps to their court appointed attorney, to lawyers, to a therapist or mental health expert in an effort to further diminish the target parent's viability as a responsible caretaker.

Has this happened in your situation? Describe how it transpired, who instigated the 'choice' scenario?

_____
_____
_____
_____
_____
_____
_____
_____
_____
_____
_____
_____
_____

ISSUE # 17

The child has made false allegations against the targeted parent in Family Court proceedings or has attempted to have the targeted parent charged criminally by police.

From 'orders of protection' to claims of abuse or neglect, it's clear how this issue is a dangerous and detrimental escalation of alienation. This includes if the child has supported such a complaint asserted by the other parent.

Often (but not always) this level of alienation and this issue in particular, points to the fact that child has been convinced to believe and even repeat what therapists call 'borrowed scenarios'. This describes how experiences that are not the child's own are 'implanted' in the child to bolster the negative image of the target parent.

In some cases its false memories of negative experiences with the target parent. In worse cases it's manufactured memories of abuse (often sexual) or neglect that never happened. A few ways this can be detected are...if the child describes (actual) experiences that transpired before the child was old enough to remember or they weren't present for. In this case the child mimics accusations advanced by the alienating parent. Such programmed untruths are not necessarily limited to the child. Often target parents experience ostracism or insult from the extended family who 'believe' the alienating parent's programmed 'story'.

Have you experienced any such accusations? Note in as much detail as possible how it happened.

_____
_____
_____
_____
_____
_____
_____
_____
_____
_____
_____
_____
_____

ISSUE # 18

The child has made (false) criminal allegations against the targeted parent to police or the court.

Note any accusations your child has leveled against you. Include the consequence in terms of orders of protection, court rulings, or arrests.

_____
_____
_____
_____
_____
_____
_____
_____
_____
_____
_____
_____
_____
_____

ISSUE # 19

The child has assaulted, attempted to harm, or harmed the target parent.

This describes any instances of violence the child has instigated against the target parent. From spitting, biting, or swearing, to physical assault this issue includes any displays of violence during contact with the target parent.

Describe any experiences of your child assaulting you in such a way.

_____
_____
_____
_____
_____
_____
_____
_____
_____
_____
_____
_____
_____

ISSUE # 20

The child has attempted suicide or engaged in self-mutilation 'because' of the targeted parent.

This issue includes any or all instances of violence toward self that the child attributes to 'harassment' by the target parent. This indicates that the child's anger and rage has turned in on itself. The emotional outrage of the whole situation has unbalanced them to the point of self-immolation the desire to end the pain by eliminating themselves.

Please understand that despite their claims no matter how loud or determined...you are not at fault. They are not doing this because of you, because you want to love them. This issue is a red alarm flare that the entire situation has grown wildly out of control. If you've avoided mental health care for yourself or child now is the time to insist.

"Cutting" and suicide attempts (no matter what the *alleged* reason) require external help from mental health professionals. No matter how difficult or unsatisfying your court experiences have been you must go directly to the courts to attempt therapeutic intervention.

Have there been claims of such self-destructive activity in your alienation experience? Describe how you 'found out'. Describe how the fact that it's 'your fault' was expressed to you. Note the situation in as much detail as possible.

_____
_____
_____
_____
_____
_____
_____
_____
_____
_____
_____
_____
_____

Ok now you've successfully logged all the details of your personal alienation experience. This is an important exercise in making sense of what's happening to you. This exercise is aimed at helping you put your experiences in some kind of manageable 'order'. As with the personal manifesto exercise, the very act of writing and recording all these details is therapeutic of itself. In addition this work is the necessary ingredient for more positive outcomes in court.

When we write (or type) we engage the logical non-emotional part of the brain. When we write about emotional, even traumatic experiences the very act of writing them alters their emotional impact and enables us to think about them slightly differently than we had before. While you may not 'magically' feel all better after recording your experiences this is the *beginning* of a transformation in your way of thinking about and processing what's happening.

Now we'll move on to look at some of the other issues.

How Could Someone Do This?

Understand the Alienator

One of the things every target parent wonders and wants to discuss when they finally begin to talk about what's happening is...'how could they do this to me'? Or 'why would they do this to me'.

Psychologists and therapists are just beginning to investigate. Dr. Craig Childress in particular has done a tremendous amount of excellent work in the psychology of alienation. But in fact, no one has all the answers. In fact few people know your alienator better than you. So the 'whys' of alienation remain obscure and personal for each case.

Some general observations point out that alienating parents are unsuccessfully struggling to recreate 'new' boundaries post-divorce. They obviously don't have the skills to maintain 'flexible' boundaries; boundaries that would allow their children to move in and out of their own personal bubble and in (and out) of the other parent's bubble without pain or confusion.

It seems their solution then is to create a hard enclosed boundary shell that keeps their children 'inside' (safe and protected) *with them*. This of course means the other parent must somehow be kept out. So the alienating parent uses their wile and skill to do whatever needs to be done to make themselves and their children 'safe' during stressful times (divorce).

The 'good news' is like anything else alienation follows the 80-20 rule. This means 80% of mild incidents of parental alienation are accidental, unintentional, and not part of a large scheme on the part of the alienator parent. This means that resolution is likely for 80% of those who recognize the early symptoms and find non-accusatory, non-threatening ways to communicate what's happening to the ex. Eighty percent of 'exes' will be surprised that their attitudes and actions are creating problems and will be willing and able to reverse the situation.

Perhaps by your thoughtful words and actions you can guarantee that your case falls into the 80% category that is resolvable.

> *Anger is the garbage of all emotion,*
> *but it takes garbage to*
> *make compost, and it takes compost*
> *to make a flower.*
> —THICH NHAT HANH

Even an otherwise fully functional human being can break down during the stress of the dissolution of a marriage and the trauma and difficulty of divorce. As you may have noticed throughout this workbook, we've done our best to minimize the use of blame, accusation, or negative finger-pointing language. This is an extremely important aspect of the healing process.

Screaming, crying, and railing against the 'perpetrator' while therapeutic during a *very small window of the process*, becomes damaging and detrimental to possible resolution in the long run. Thinking about them, talking about them as 'evil,' 'crazy,' or 'nuts' may help you vent some of your anger ***initially***…but once such thinking becomes entrenched, what you end up thinking and believing is ultimately the same as what they are doing to you.

Thinking of them as the enemy, as a destructive force, using negative language even only to yourself can become so habitual you end up slipping and saying something negative in front of your children. Then you become no different from them and push possible resolution further out of reach.

It may be a challenge. It may not be what you want to hear or wish to realize but in order to overcome the consequences of escalating alienation you, the 'the one feeling victimized', need to become the 'bigger' person. Whatever your role in the former marriage or in the devolution of the marriage, or even in the divorce, once you start being alienated your role becomes re-defined. Now clearly if you react in anger, your anger will be used against you.

You can't solve or resolve the situation by being mean*er*, angri*er*, *more* manipulative, *more* destructive, or *more* vehement. You won't solve the situation by only hiring the most expensive attorneys and plunging into an extended (expensive) court battle. You won't solve the problem by only dragging your children or your ex into court or into forced mental health testing or therapy. While lawyers and judges may be a part of the solution, while therapy may be another part of a long term solution- it's not all in their hands.

We've talked to literally hundreds of parents at different stages of alienation and not once have we heard that one day in court magically resolved it all. In fact quite the contrary, a court battle tends to exacerbate and further polarize the parties causing financial strain and emotional strife.

Alienation is your call to evolve to become the kind of person who can be calm in the face of the worst kind of abuse. Think of Martin Luther King's lunch counter children. Think of the violence, degradation, and abuse such pioneers on the forefront of a cause faced. You are on the forefront of a newly discovered form of intentional, highly targeted marginalization, organized prejudice and discrimination. The question becomes: 'How will you rise to the occasion'?

Managing Yourself & Your Emotions

Anger

Of all the parents we speak with...almost all of them struggle with this overwhelming, sometimes blinding emotion. We are not psychologists or counselors and make no claims to be such, so please take these comments and observations in the light of experience in which they are offered. I (Jill) only dare to speak about such things because of the sheer need I see. Dozens, sometimes hundreds, of hurting parents contact me weekly after hearing my radio show or seeing local broadcasts of my show 'Family Matters'. I (Jill) base my conclusions, comments, and observations on the thousands of conversations I've had with individuals, experts, and in my support group.

It should be no surprise that the first most obvious emotion parents on the alienation carousel confront is anger. It doesn't take a scientist to realize that living engulfed in anger is toxic and dangerous; dangerous to one's health, dangerous to one's emotional well-being, and perhaps most important of all dangerous to one's relationships. If you get stuck in the anger it can make resolving the situation nearly impossible. If you get stuck in the anger you can find yourself trapped in a very lonely, unsatisfying life.

If we're not careful...anger can destroy us.

Here's a quick quiz to help you determine if you should seek professional help to manage it:

Anger Quiz

Answer yes or no to the following questions. Base your answers on how you've behaved over the past year. If you *suspect* that you have an anger management problem seek professional help regardless of your score on this. If you *think* you *might* you're probably right. Answer yes or no to the following questions.

1. I don't get angry about everything that makes me mad but if I do – look out.

   _____

2. I get angry *still* if I think of things that hurt me in the past.

    _____

3. Waiting in line, or for other people, really get me mad.

    ____NO____

4. I 'fly off the handle' (raise my voice, shout, yell, demonstrate) more than once a week.

    _____

5. I have heated arguments with those closest to me.

    _____

6. I lie awake at night thinking about the things that upset me during the day or in the past.

    _____

7. When someone upsets me I don't *usually* say anything but I spend a lot of time thinking up cutting replies I should have said.

    _____

8. I find forgiving someone who has done me wrong incredibly difficult.

   _____

9. When I lose control of my emotions I get angry with myself.

   _____

10. When people don't behave the way they should they really irritate me.

    _____

11. Getting really upset makes me feel sick later, in the form of weakness, headaches, or upset stomach.

    _____

12. People I've trusted have betrayed me leaving me angry.

    _____

13. I get depressed when things don't go my way.

    _____

14. When I get frustrated I can't put it out of my mind.

    _____

15. I have been so angry I can't remember what I said or did in my rage.

_____

16. After I argue with someone I'm incredibly mad at myself.

_____

17. I've had trouble at work because of my temper.

_____

18. When riled I can blurt things I later regret.

_____

19. People have told me they are afraid of my bad temper.

_____NO_____

20. If I get angry, frustrated or hurt I feel better by eating, drinking alcohol or using other drugs.

_____

21. If someone hurts me I want to get even.

_____

22. I've gotten so angry that I've become violent, hitting people or breaking things.

_____ No

23. There have been times I've felt angry enough 'to kill'.

_____ No

24. I've felt so hurt and alone that I've considered suicide.

_____

25. I'm an angry person. I know I need help because anger has already caused me a lot of problems.

_____

If you answered 'yes' to 10 or more questions, or if you answered 'yes' to any of the last 4 questions - you should seek treatment. If you've answered 'yes' to fewer than 5 questions you're in control of your anger better than most people.

Scores on this test are not meant to be any kind of diagnosis tool! As we said earlier, neither Michele nor myself are healthcare professionals. This quiz is here only to provide some ideas for self-reflection. Always consult with a trained mental health professional if you experience feelings or thoughts that you'd describe as 'out of control'. If you are having thoughts about hurting someone or about suicide seek *immediate* treatment from mental health professional.

What is Anger?

Anger and Fear

Fear lies behind anger even if the angry person appears to be strong and in control. In fact, most anger springs out of a deep fear. Anger is the harvest of failed expectations. When we're angry, it usually means we are or something or someone close to us is being threatened. In the case of alienation it's of course the looming threat of losing our connection with our children. We try to replace the strong, negative feeling; fear, with a different negative emotion; anger.

Anger masquerades as power to counteract powerlessness. It operates like a pharmaceutical chemical and functions to mask pain while generating energy. It feels better to be enraged than impotent. Humans' greatest fears focus on what's unknown, on things we don't understand. In part because our minds have the capacity to 'anticipate' a worst case scenario for any possible situation...this creates fear. And at the moment parental alienation is still a large 'unknown'. When we don't understand something we fear it will rob us of something we hold dear. Fear, more often than not, creates anger.

Anger arises when we don't have a way to put the energy of our fear to work somehow, which is why activism is such a useful pursuit for a target parent. Anger feels like a weapon we can use against the source of our fears but truly it's an obstacle that can affect our entire life.

Angry people fear something. Angry target parents fear the loss of their connection to their children. Anger is a normal human response to a tense or threatening environment or situation that triggers the 'fight or flight' response. This sends a surge of chemicals from the nervous system into the body which causes increase respiration and dilates blood vessels. This is why anger is so detrimental to us. We naturally get angry if our freedom, our ideas, ideals, relationships, etc. are threatened. This is especially true in intimate relationships where anger and fear become personal, and way more serious.

Anger is so easy to ignite, and hard to defuse. It is the most destructive of emotions, and one of the hardest to handle. Anger can lead to physical violence, property destruction, and other damage ranging in severity from the disappointing to devastating. But most of all; your anger plays right into the hands of the alienating parent.

All of us experience this normal emotion called anger. Some people vent, others resort to attacks, and still others suppress their anger. The truth is anger affect us in three ways; in our physical body, in our thoughts, and by influencing our behavior.

Becoming angry doesn't 'just happen'. It's rooted in how we think; our thought process. How we evaluate each situation we experience determines how we feel and behave. If you think you're being cheated, exploited, betrayed, or treated unfairly the most obvious reaction is to become angry. The way anger is expressed varies from person to person. The consequences range from acts of violence to total suppression of anger.

Although anger is a normal emotion it's very misunderstood. We are taught anger is an 'inappropriate' emotion. Children often hear, "Don't you talk that way to me!" The message is that children are not expected - nor do they have the right - to become angry. But venting sometimes leads to violence. Suppressing anger over a sustained period leads to heart disease, etc. For many, the alienation situation may be their first opportunity to recognize and express decades of repressed, accumulated anger. For perhaps the first time, people have a mouthpiece—a lawyer. In the courtroom I (Judge Michele) often see anger far out of proportion to the generating offense. It's obvious when accumulated, 'historical' anger is at play, it's hyper-destructive. Historical anger carries an exaggerated charge that's difficult to hone in on because it's existed for so long. This entrenched anger is often expressed inappropriately.

As I say in the anger chapter of my book "The Good Karma Divorce":

Anger can have an amphetamine-like effect offering a powerful surge of energy. It increases confidence and motivation and induces a false sense of power. Empowered by anger, we are also able to resist giving in to sadness. As anger releases adrenaline into our system, we are no longer sad and sluggish, but motivated into action. Practically speaking, anger is the default emotion that prevents us from feeling weak. We all know how inarticulate we can become when we are angry. Our pulse races and we feel we must do something. When this is our mental state, we can't say what we really mean. We say more than we want to, and we say it with a mean spirit. Ambrose Bierce, the journalist and short-story author, captured it when he said, "Speak when you are angry and you will make the best speech you will ever regret."

The anger impulse is firmly grounded in primitive brain. The primitive limbic system is an automatic response forged long before our thinking brain developed the ability to cultivate thought and use logic. If a negative or angry thought has no outlet, it feeds back into the mind and creates an even more anxious thought. Which is why anger is so hard to escape from once the feeling overwhelms us.

Scientists have found that replaying negative thoughts enables the brain to enlarge its receptors increasing the individuals' sensitivity to a particular emotion. Reducing or reframing anger creates positive bonds that seem to trigger neuroplastic change by unlearning and dissolving negative neuronal networks.

When we change our attitude about our anger, different neurons will fire in the brain, upgrading our brain chemistry, its function, and vitality.

The Price of Anger

Sustained anger will wear you out. The more you depend on anger the more it will exhaust you. Researchers at the University of North Carolina have found that those who express anger verbally or physically are likely to have high levels of cholesterol. They found that men and women with higher anger levels had higher levels of homocystine, a chemical strongly associated with heart disease, in the blood. Studies of the bodily responses during anger found our bodies flood with adrenaline. Some of the physical consequences include heart disease, increase in blood pressure, and constriction of blood vessels in the digestive track.

In this state, we are overcome by a tidal wave of chemicals flooding our body. Who hasn't been willing to risk everything to say what was on our mind? A small voice in our head may shout, "Don't say it. Just don't say it", but we are unable to stop. The surge of adrenaline inspires such a behavioral imperative. The chemicals are actually doing the talking at such times; while our brains take a backseat. This chemical wave tells us we will feel better if we unleash the venom. Robert Sapolsky says that anger chemicals, cortisol and glucocorticoids, are destructive in the human body if they remain for an extended period. They can, over time, impair the function of the immune and endocrine systems.

These may suggest how dangerous anger is to toy with and therefore may suggest that suppression is the only answer. But suppressing anger isn't healthy either. Research shows that those who suppress or 'refuse to deal with' it, and seethe inside, are at an elevated risk for coronary heart disease. Burying anger can lead to self-loathing, anxiety, and physical and emotional symptoms.

How then do we express anger in a healthy manner when we see the world through a red-hot lens when angry? It becomes difficult for an angry person to think rationally. Often leading to regret about what we said or how we behaved in the "heat of the moment" because our brains were unable to function properly. Trying to determine the healthiest way to deal with anger is hard but far from impossible.

When we're angry at someone or something, we give them power over us. When we allow someone else to make us angry it's because we feel they are a threat.

Anger management is more than controlling your breath or counting from one to ten. To truly curb and manage chronic anger requires a deep understanding of your fear. Anger is fear. If you can manage your fears it will be easier for you to manage your anger.

The best way to handle with anger then is to deal with it.

In my book, "The Good Karma Divorce", I offer some tools not only for diffusing anger but for personal transformation. In the section "Anger: Miraculous Things Can Happen in the Mud", I provide some way to get some distance from your anger.

Anger cannot heal the heart; healing the heart takes a different kind of attention. An alternative approach to anger includes a little compassion for yourself. To create a little space that can allow your anger to wane. In that space the chemical load of will reduce. Although you may not change your mind you have made space of a different outcome.

Not reacting when triggered and creating that space before reacting are easier said than done. The eighth-century Indian monk Shantideva refers to it as 'reframing your attitude toward discomfort'. To do this requires you to just sit with that angry feeling without the need to do something about it. The more you repeat a reaction, you reinforce that reaction; you strengthen those neuropathways, so that they speed you to a better reaction. The more often you react in anger or resentment, the more heightened your susceptibility is to different irritations and eventually even to minor ones.

Each time you cause someone harm even in anger you may well be picking up a little karmic debt you don't want to have to repay. Leaving space gives you a window to watch your behavior and say to yourself, "Yes, I can see that". When you look at your anger objectively you gain the ability to uncover the strength beneath. That is where true power is. You can choose to do this any time you confront anger.

The question becomes...are you more committed to being wise or to being right? We are multifaceted: sometimes we are right, sometimes wrong, and sometimes a mixture; we overreact or under react. There is no perfection—we are all contradictory and inconsistent, illogical, hypocritical, paradoxical, and unpredictable. It is part of the nature of being human. Accepting this is an act of self-compassion. As we come to accept this we come closer to accepting ourselves. We'll also be less angry when someone else demonstrates the same imperfections. The Novelist Marcel Proust, was devoted to exploring the many dimensions of personality. The value of his exercise is to help you become more comfortable with the ambiguity of truth. It's designed to get you to change the way you look at things, to redefine your mental ground rules. The aim is...to change your susceptibility to anger.

Tip #1 • A Proustian exercise:

Make a list of the last five things that made you angry and give two 'different' interpretations beyond your original one. One of the interpretations may be from the others' point of view. As you do this recognize how this applies to every situation you experience day to day.

From this exercise you can begin to see that your 'interpretation' of any situation can never be 100 percent correct. For example, a father brings the children home an hour *and a half late from visitation. The mother was furious, she felt "disrespected" and believed he was demonstrating how he could flaught court orders.*

Of course other potential interpretations could be: (1) he found it difficult to separate from the children; or (2) the children caused delay to spend more time with him. Note how this exercise disarms your hair trigger.

What (I think) happened:

_____
_____
_____
_____
_____
_____
_____
_____
_____
_____
_____
_____
_____
_____
_____

Re-interpretation #1

_____
_____
_____
_____
_____
_____
_____
_____
_____
_____
_____
_____
_____

Re-interpretation #2

_____
_____
_____
_____
_____
_____
_____
_____
_____
_____
_____
_____
_____

Tip #2 • *Writing a letter*

Write a letter that you never intend to send to the person you are angry at. Be as irate as you need to, but do try to express the emotions (fear, insecurity, abandonment) behind your anger. Include it all, every built up resentment that's accumulated. Dumping your emotions on the page affords your brain access different neuro pathways so you can consider your anger more objectively. Writing lets you feel you've 'done something' with your anger other despite reacting against the one who caused it. After you're done destroy the letter.

Dear _____

I need to let you know that I'm furious about...

_____
_____
_____
_____
_____
_____
_____
_____
_____
_____
_____
_____
_____
_____
_____
_____
_____
_____
_____
_____

Tip #3 • Share With a Designated 'Listener'

Vent your anger to a close friend. Choose someone who has nothing to do with your situation, who's not involved with your family. One cautionary note: check with this person before you begin. Be sure it is a safe and convenient time for them to listen. If not plan for a better time and talk then. Be sure you choose a good listener, someone who doesn't incite you to further anger or mire you in more negativity. If your 'listener' friend has an emotional reaction to what you're describing they may be reacting from their own experiences and not offering the objectivity you need. Take note to whether you feel more agitated or more tired after your chat. If the answer is yes, you may need to check before you decide to have another conversation with that person.

Tip #4 • Make A "Hit List"

Write a list of all the people you're angry at, past and present, and explain note why. See if any offenses have been duplicated. Your alienation situation may be reactivating past offenses in your life that may exaggerate your responses to those situations.

Who   Why

_____ _____

_____ _____

_____ _____

_____   _____

_____   _____

_____   _____

Tip #5 • Listen With A Different Ear

Next time someone else is demonstrating anger at you listen until they are finished talking. Ask if they're done before you speak. Consider whether there is anything justified in their assertion. If so, take responsibility for the justified part. If they are at the peak of their anger don't try to calm them down. They won't be physically able to calm down until they have finished venting or have exhausted their adrenaline. Practice having conversations with people where you hear them out no matter what they are saying. Start this practice with 'benign' conversations, chats you aren't really invested in. It will be much easier to do.

Another approach is 'meditative listening'. Focus completely on what the other person is saying. Listen and breathe especially what they say agitates. Strive to not think about what fabulous response you will make when they're finally done talking. Focus on the breathing as intently as you focus on what's being said.

I (Judge Michele) learned one other approach to deflecting anger from a Jesuit priest that you can also do while you are listening. He taught that we should pray for our enemies. The act of praying or meditating helps release some of the sting of the anger.

Tip #6 • Walk

One timeless solution to anger is...go for a walk. Walking is a highly effective technique for dissipating the biological effects of anger. Even during negotiations or a trial, I (Judge Michele) may suggest that the litigants and lawyers take a ten minute walk. Anger pumps adrenaline through the system. Research has indicated that a walk can dissipate these 'stress' chemicals and produce chemical pain relievers that promote relaxation.

According to Dr. John Ratey walking releases tryptophan and other feel-good endorphins into the bloodstream which will stabilize moods. When you walk, your heart increases blood flow throughout your body releasing stress from the muscles. Your joints release a lubricating fluid that eases body tension. If you walk outside there is an increase of oxygen in the brain. A well-oxygenated brain enhances clarity. Of course any exercise will have the same beneficial effect. But sometimes we're too angry to exercise so walk instead.

Tip #7 • Meditation- Relaxation

Thousands of books have been written about the value of meditation. It decreases confusion, enhances clarity, instills calm, orders chaotic thinking, and clears the mind. If you do it, it will deliver. Master some method of relaxation so you can use it anytime you need to calm down. Breathe deep. As you exhale imagine the bottled-up fury being released from your nose and mouth. Let it go and be free. Repeat this over and again until you feel peaceful. Then visualize being in a place where you've been happy.

It may be a beach, garden, or anywhere that comes to mind. Just imagine being there and inhaling the essence of your serene environment. This will help you regain your inner peace.

Tip #8 • *Realize That Anger Fades*

Make a list of five things in your life that you were very, very angry about that no longer mean as much (or anything) to you. As you make this list, you will realize that what is angering you now is just another one of the things that will shortly lose its intensity.

1.

_____
_____
_____
_____
_____
_____
_____
_____
_____
_____
_____
_____
_____

2.

3.

4.

_____
_____
_____
_____
_____
_____
_____
_____
_____
_____
_____
_____

5.

_____
_____
_____
_____
_____
_____
_____
_____
_____
_____
_____
_____
_____

When you heat metal the molecular integrity of the metal gets stronger. Each time you come back from conflict in a positive way, you become more resilient. To allow for disagreement is to allow the other people to be them self. People will at times let you down. In fact, almost everyone will disappoint you at one time or another. Those closest to you will behave badly from time to time but we must offer others the same understanding you need from time to time.

Anger-management classes teach that repressing anger is not effective. Enhancing compassion is far more successful in the process of decreasing anger. To be compassionate is to be understanding and gentle with another person who is struggling.

15 Ways to Keep Anger From Impacting Your Case

Emotions build. Each time your visitation is interfered with will have a cumulative effect that may make you hyper sensitive. This can magnify things that may not warrant the attention they're getting or may not warrant the degree of response even when they do require a response.

As I (Judge Michele) stated before, filing a petition is a rational thing to do and as you write and rewrite your document you give your thoughts breathing time. Acting spontaneously in your anger is just going to make things worse. You run the risk of having an Order of Protection against you. One tactic the alienator uses is to blow tiny things out of proportion to obtain an Order of Protection.

Before you take any action first look at the consequences of your amped up anger; have you written emails, make hostile phone calls, yelled at your child, become overly aggressive, or has anger pushed you to retreat and do nothing. You must separate what is true from the triggered emotions.

The path of destructive anger and victim thinking weakens us. When you show that anger in court you risk losing credibility. I have had many cases where the target parent looked unbalanced and the alienator was coherent and articulate. Remember the judge only has a snapshot of the situation.

In the seventeen years I have been serving in the court in domestic relations I have learned and want to share with you these counterintuitive tips for reducing stress and giving you back some power.

To test if your anger **serves** you ask yourself the following questions;

1. Are you absolutely certain what you think is true?

2. Make a list of any evidence there is to support the anger?

3. Does this anger further your constructive goals?

4. Does this anger degenerate your relationship with your children?

5. In what ways does this anger help you?

6. In what ways does this anger help your spouse?

When speaking to others when you are upset or angry keep these in mind:

1. It is important that you acknowledge your own accountability no matter how small.

2. See what you can learn by asking the other person what their hurtful words meant.

3. Slow down your reactions by checking if your old habits are exacerbating the conflict.

4. When you ask a question of your former spouse do so to find out information not to infer your agenda or to prove them wrong. A question is to gather information not to send subtle messages. If you have an agenda, once they sense it, then it is easy for them to get power by refusing you.

5. When you press someone to agree with you, you can strengthen their resistance.

6. After you have been criticized you might say, "It feels like you are being really critical of me, but I'm not in a mood to take it personally." (That statement is a little devilish, as it really frustrates the criticizer.)

7. Remember, you are not the warden of your former spouse's behavior, so you don't have to scold, lecture, or sound like a disciplinarian.

8. The word *should* is usually quite judgmental and usually makes people defensive.

9. Tone—on the phone, in the home, or in a neutral zone—makes or breaks the effect. Say this statement nicely: "You were always a very loving, generous husband." Now say the same statement sarcastically. You get the picture.

10. Acknowledge how defensive your statements MAY BE.

11. When your ex-spouse is speaking, don't interrupt.

    a. Your interruption will make them feel disrespected.

    b. You won't hear what you need to hear.

    c. They will be too offended to actually 'hear' what you are saying. The greater the emotional extreme the less people hear.

12. You can't make people see sense when they are in the crescendo of their anger.

13. Eye contact, facial expressions, and gestures count: after all 51% of brain is dedicated to visual processing.

14. Whoever asks the questions controls the communication so ask open-ended questions such as: 'What happened next?'

15. The word 'why' makes people psychologically defensive. Instead of asking 'why' ask: 'What brought you to that decision?'

Shame & Guilt

Guilt and shame are powerful emotions associated with the parental alienation experience. Parents often feel guilty possibly for very real reasons; such as...how they contributed to the degradation of the marriage. This is especially true if in some way their actions toppled the house of cards that was the marriage. It's natural to feel guilty even if we weren't the person 'at fault'. We feel guilt and shame for being part of a failure. We feel guilt and shame for things we 'should have' done or ways we should have acted. We feel guilty because we're human and we make mistakes then we feel ashamed of failing, ashamed for having failed at marriage, for having failed at being the parent you hoped to be.

There's so much guilt and so much shame and it's such heartbreak in our lives. Just trying to watch a simple sports game on television or on a documentary on TV and we see commercials of happy families everywhere. But when you don't have your family you just feel outside of that world and it hurts and that's OK. You're not alone.

We can do work together to try to resolve it. One of the biggest problems with getting stuck or being weighted down with shame and guilt is that it drives people to give up. Guilt and shame tend to push alienated parents right over the edge. Their own guilt and shame is such a burden that they simply cannot sustain the fight against ex-spouse, can't confront the propaganda. They can't fight against the subtle origins of alienation and if the legal onslaught should pile on top they just give up and give up in. While there are other reasons people give up, guilt is one of them.

Getting stuck in guilt and shame often leads alienated parents to lose out on that relationship, lose out on that that part of their lives. They might risk their opportunities to turn it around again unless they're willing to take a more active role.

Another way guilt and shame have a negative impact on the alienated parent's fight is that guilt and shame keep us from sharing our burden with anyone outside our family. In some cases it happens even inside our family, because alienation tends to tear entire families apart. We have in-laws and sisters on one side and aunts and cousins lining up on the other side and gets very complicated and it gets very unpleasant. Shame and guilt are often the emotions that keep us from reaching out and trying to find people who are willing to help us through our darkest times. Because of shame and guilt we wind up being alone. Usually what happens is isolation which inhibits healing.

You can see how these negative emotions can be a problem for anyone in a situation like this. Going it alone can be overwhelming, in fact this alone-ness that many alienated parents feel is one of the reasons that I decided to get active through writing my (Jill) book (*The Look of Love*). I became convinced that we need to speak out about what was happening to so many parents and above all find solutions.

Guilt & Shame Exercise

Take a moment now to jot down all the ways that you feel guilty or you feel responsible for what's happening to you.

_____
_____
_____
_____
_____
_____
_____
_____
_____
_____
_____
_____

List the mistakes you think you have made. Which of those mistakes you feel bad about may not have been your fault? Now, what mistakes have you really made? What issues have you actually caused? Ask yourself how are you a part of the problem?

Just list these for now. I'm not trying to make you keep a list of the things that you think are challenging about yourself but the purpose of this exercise is to help you see how hard you may be on yourself, or how unavoidable those mistakes may have been. It is possible you are being harder on yourself than ever the alienating parent could be?

_____
_____
_____
_____
_____
_____
_____
_____
_____
_____
_____
_____

The point of writing these down is solely so you can just let yourself feel, and realize and understand what exactly you do feel guilty about. Once you do this you're in a position to separate the reality from the overblown, exaggerated, bundled together fears that tend to build up when we refuse to truly 'look at' our less than delightful emotions.

On the bench I (Judge Michele) have found that few divorces leave the participants without some nagging remorse about what could have been done to prevent it. That's why I included my view of guilt in "The Good Karma Divorce."

As we scan our behavior, we may decide that we were saints, but this is rare. If we hurt someone we once loved or our family, it may feel like a violation of our core values, which can give rise to shame and guilt. Guilt serves as an obstacle to keep us from moving out of pain, because it traps us in our melodrama about how much we have hurt someone else. Extended guilt is destructive, because it erodes self-worth. To maintain self-worth, we often engage in either denial and withdrawal or an immense amount of overcompensation directed at the people we think we have wronged. Because of the elusive quality of guilt, we do too much or too little to try to reduce it; it has an insatiable appetite, and it is hard to gauge the right amount to feed it.

To help you gauge this we ask you to separate the real from the exaggerated you can start to let go, to not wallow in the feelings that disempower you and drag you down.

Now jot down all the things that you feel terrible about, mistakes, problems, the role you've played in the worst problems. Write down the worst things you've done in your marriage, to your children's, and/or spouse. Really dig in and be brave and write things down here. (It is for a reason).

_____
_____
_____
_____
_____
_____
_____
_____
_____
_____
_____
_____
_____

Now take a good long look at those things...and consider what in your mind would be the rightful punishment for all those things? What would somebody who did those things really deserve?

_____
_____
_____
_____
_____
_____
_____
_____
_____
_____
_____
_____
_____
_____

Would such a person *really* deserve to **never** see there are children again? Would they even deserve to have a broken, impaired relationship with their children?

_____

_____

Of course not! Almost no one deserves that! Of course you would never pass that sentence on to someone else knowing what you've gone through...so why pass that judgment on yourself when you know that you may not deserve it?

Although we don't know you individually we do know that alienated parents often feel they are bad. This is usually far from true. From one alienated parent (Jill) to another, I want to tell you that you are not a bad person, you are not a terrible human being, and you don't deserve what is happening to you. For so many people it is not 100 percent your fault, in fact it usually never is.

In our (Jill) support group, so many of our adult alienated children are coming to the meetings to tell us stories about how hard it was, how difficult the alienation situation was during their childhood. When they describe how much of an impact this situation made, how alienation really adversely affected their lives in so very many ways.

You are entitled to your relationship with your child without interference from your ex-spouse no matter who was responsible for the divorce, no matter who was at fault. There is nothing wrong with you and I just wanted to point that out because I (Jill) know this first-hand how enduring alienation can be a crazy making experience but don't let anyone convince you this is something you deserve because it's not true.

Parenting

A Parenting Plan

First let me note that your parenting rights will be more stable, more protected if you and your ex have what's called a "Parenting Agreement", a "Joint Parenting Agreement" or ideally a "Shared Parenting Agreement" on file with the courts. We included some of the most important points of a strong agreement so you can get an overview of the possibilities no matter what legal form your agreement might take. A strong shared agreement should detail all of the obligations and responsibilities of both parties very clearly. It should be endorsed and it is considered a binding court order.

If you don't have one – if possible— get one in place right away. Shared parenting guidelines are one of the best possible preventative measures, one of the best ways for preventing potential alienation before it starts. A parenting plan should cover all eventualities; such as what happens to visitation times if children are sick, how to handle doctors' visits how to handle holidays.

A good plan will eliminate many of the potential loopholes for alienation; i.e. it will be harder to change visit times at the last minute without consequences, it will be more difficult to use medical excuses without consequences. A thoughtful and carefully drafted plan is the best tool for harmonious post-divorce parenting.

The workbook contains an extremely good example and having one of these in place is the best way to prevent alienation:

41 Points A Parenting Plan Should Address

Please note that most of these clauses may also be used in sole custody parenting plans. Not all clauses are going to be applicable to every situation, but they are here for you to consider and pick and choose. **These suggestions also serve for topics for you to go over with your attorney, and know that many of these suggestions are *ideal*, but not always attainable.**

1. The children/child's name. The agreement should specify that the child will keep the last name of the target parent.

2. If previous visitation has been denied the court may adopt temporary visitation to make up for the lost time.

3. Agreement should state whether supervision is required at visitation.

4. Include where the visit(s) will take place, i.e. in a neutral, public place, the father's home, the mother's etc.

5. How long each visitation will last. i.e. 'for 3 hours, each visit', 'for one overnight stay.'

6. Which Parent shall drive the children to and from each visit. i.e.

   a. At the beginning of the visit Father drives to Mother's location

   b. Mother drives to Father's location at the end of the visit.

7. How Parenting Time will be divided during regular school days:

   a. Mother/Father will have parenting time with said children from after school Thursday to Monday before school begins. Many jurisdictions have traditional alternating weekends and one day in the week.

   b. Make sure that order is more specific than 'every other weekend.' This gets confusing and police won't enforce it. Put for example 'the first and third weekend of every month.'

c. The residential parent shall provide clothing and small child favorite toy and that clothing and toy will return be at next visit.

8. Special Holiday schedules should be clear. Don't forget to include the lesser 'holidays' like Spring Break from school, Labor Day, Memorial Day, Fathers' Day, Mothers' Day, Parent's birthday, child's birthday, other family member birthdays.

   a. On even/odd years, Father/Mother shall have the children on the following occasions. On odd years, Mother shall have the children on the following occasions.

   b. Easter: 6:00 pm Friday preceding Easter until 6:00 pm Sunday.

   c. July 4: 6:00 pm July 3 until 6:00 pm on July 5.

   d. 6:00 pm the Wednesday preceding Thanksgiving until 6:00 pm Sunday.

9. Summer is often divided or two to six weeks for non residential Parent.

   a. For the purpose of summer vacations, each Parent shall be allowed a two (2) week uninterrupted period of Parenting Time with children.

   b. Each Parent shall inform the other Parent, in writing, of the dates of his/her vacation with the children no later than May 1st of each year.

10. It's a good idea to add a 'conflicts clause' that determines that Special days and Holidays shall prevail over regular periods of Parenting Time.

11. Who is responsible for making day care provisions and when.

    a. The Parent who children are staying with shall be responsible for daily care for children.

12. Make provisions for major medical decisions and general welfare decisions:

    a. Include dental, psychiatric, tattoos, body piercing or other alterations.

    b. Passport application, name change, signing of contracts on behalf of said children must be made by prior written consent of both parties or further order of the Court.

13. Include a clause that defines who is to have communications with all doctors, clinics, school nurses, counselors, and others that are involved in the health and welfare of said children.

    a. Each Parent shall permit and encourage communications by the other Parent with the child care provider if necessary.

14. Who has access to important documents:

    a. Each party shall see that ALL records for children are available to both parties.

    b. Each Parent shall be provided with copies of the Birth Certificate and Social Security cards of each of said children within [x] days of this order.

15. Include provisions for unexpected illness.

    a. Each Parent shall provide twelve (12) hours advance notification to the other Parent of any illness or accident requiring medical attention.

    b. Within two (2) hours of any life threatening illness or accident.

    c. Each Parent shall immediately notify the other in the event of the death of said children.

16. How changes to the agreement should be handled.

    a. Modifications by mutual agreement must be in writing, dated, signed and witnessed, and each Parent shall retain a copy.

17. Define the telephone, text, IM, video conference, etc. access each parent will have. And of course any 'house rules' for appropriate times to call, and how much age appropriate privacy the children will be allowed for phone/computer, etc.

    a. Father/Mother shall have the right to buy a cell phone for child for the purpose of phone calls, emergency contact and texting.

    b. Communication with children including but not limited to four, thirty minute telephone calls per week or may be once on a daily basis.

    c. Not between the hours of 11:00 pm and 7:00 am, except in cases of emergency.

    d. Neither party shall interfere with the children's privacy during telephone conversations, etc.

18. An agreement might include who is responsible for the expense of transportation and when.

   a. In some cases each Parent shall provide half of all transportation.

   b. The Father, or an authorized agent, shall pick children up when they are at Mothers home, and the Mother, or an authorized agent, shall pick children up when they are at Father's home.

19. Who will use claim the tax deductions for the children when.

   a. The Father/Mother shall exercise the Federal and State dependency tax deductions with reference to [child's name] each and every year/ every other year until said child reaches the age of 19.

20. What should happen if a Parent must travel during their visitation time.

   a. If either Parent leaves the children for forty-eight (48) hours or more, that Parent will offer the other Parent the additional time before making other arrangements.

   b. The Parent shall notify the other Parent of temporary care of children by other persons.

21. Clearly outline when a missed visit will require make up time.

   a. Should one Parent not be able to exercise his/her entire Parenting/vacation time, make-up time shall be agreed on in writing in advance by both parents.

b. Makeup visitation; should be scheduled within 14 days.

22. Clearly indicate who will have access to vital information.

   a. Each Parent will give the other the telephone number and address where the children live, and notify the other party in advance of any changes of address and/or telephone number for the children.

   b. Each party will give the name, address, and telephone number of the daycare, preschool, or school, church, or contact person for any activity or program the children attend.

23. A Parenting Agreement should include a clause defining who the child will be with.

   a. Each Parent will inform the other party of the names of all non-related persons living with or visiting the children's residence for more than three/ two/ one week(s).

24. How and when the parents should contact each other.

   a. Each party shall not contact the employer(s) of the other party for any reason whatsoever.

   b. During work hours any contact with the other parent should be limited to emergency contact regarding the urgent health and welfare of said children.

25. The agreement should spell out how to handle sleep-overs or trips with other friends or family.

   a. The Parents shall provide the address and telephone number of where the children will stay for 24 hours/2 days or more.

26. Who makes decisions about school?

   a. School, shall be approved by the Parents jointly.

27. What will happen if the child is required to attend summer school?

   a. Should children be required to attend school during the summer vacation, children shall attend school at the location of the Father/Mother.

28. Under what circumstances parenting time can be changed or not changed.

   a. Parenting Time will NOT be changed because that child is: busy, not available, are being punished, are suffering an illness, or refuse to go.

   b. The receiving Parent will have the option of caring for the child during illness unless under the care of a physician for serious illness.

31. The Parent in possession of the child shall not allow the Step-Parent to administer corporal punishment or strike the children for any reason.

32. What is considered out of bounds behavior in front of the children.

a. Mother/Father are restrained from harassing, annoying, striking with hand or object, threatening, assaulting, using verbally abusive language, or molesting the other Parent or Step-Parent in any manner in the presence of said children, during phone calls or at any other time.

33. That Parenting Time is protected time.

   a. The parties shall not plan or arrange any event or opportunity whatsoever during the other Parent's scheduled parenting time.

   b. That the parties shall not allow or attempt to persuade said children to ask for or demand an alternate or reduced parenting time.

34. In the event of death of either Parent, full legal and physical custody of said children shall be retained by the surviving Parent.

35. Who is responsible for providing medical insurance and medical expenses.

   a. Each Parent shall provide the other with all medical insurance information, including a copy of the insurance card.

   b. In the event that one or both Parents do NOT have medical insurance, the Parents will agree to medical insurance and split the cost fifty-fifty.

c. The Parents will split the cost of all medical, pharmaceutical, dental, dental, eye care, or any other physical or mental health expenses not covered by insurance fifty-fifty.

d. The Parent who incurs the bill should submit a copy of that bill and explanation of benefits to the other Parent within 45 days to receive payment.

e. The other Parent will submit their portion of that payment to the other Parent within 30 days.

36. Special provisions if visitation interference occurs.

a. Include a court order of visitation or parenting plan violations.

i. The Court also finds that Mother/Father has had difficulty in observing this rule thus far, and that such prior violations have warranted the implementation of this present Order.

37. Define what constitutes a violation of the Parenting Plan.

a. A violation of the Parenting Plan is defined as any delay or failure to produce the child(ren) for visitation to the other parent, or failure to have the children available for the scheduled telephonic contact between the minor children and the absent parent.

b. Delay is defined as being in excess of 30 minutes late for a scheduled transfer or telephonic contact, without a verifiable extraordinary excuse.

38. Include the consequences of any violation of the Parenting Plan.

    a. Violations of any part of the visitation or communication plan at any time will result in the graduated sanctions listed below.

    b. In the event that three visits have been missed, the (Target Parent) and child shall attend therapy together without the father/mother having to petition the court.

        i. Father/Mother may choose the therapist or if the child is already in therapy the mother/father can decide to use that therapist if it meets the approval of that therapist.

    c. If more than two visits are canceled in a period of two months the mother/father shall be entitled to double Parenting Time. If two visits are canceled in a row then father/mother has the right to 4 visits.

    d. In the event that three visit are canceled by mother/father without good cause shown in addition to all the other relief she shall pay $100 per missed visit.

    e. Any party found to have violated the Parenting Time order she shall be responsible for both parties' attorneys' fees.

39. What should happen is one Parent is hostile in front of the children.

    a. If custodial or residential Parent is hostile or argues in front of the child either parent shall have the right to discretely [not seen by the children] bring a audio recorder or mp3 to the interaction and such recordings shall be admissible in court.

40. Include what will happen if abuse claims are made.

    a. If mother/father (alienating parent) claims abuse of any kind the child shall be brought to a doctor within three days to verify the abuse. (This prevents getting caught up in the court system where the court usually must error on the side of the child.)

41. Include any other special individual provisions.

    a. The child[ren] shall keep a picture of the other Parent in their room.

    b. Child shall not refer to any other male as 'father' or any other female as 'mother.'

    c. All gifts and letters and phone messages shall be tendered to the child from the target Parent and their relatives.

10 Super Parenting Skills

Once parents get some idea about where they are along the continuum from mild to moderate to severe; once a parent understands how to deal with the anger or how to manage the guilt or shame they're feeling....the most urgent issue they want to discuss is how to parent under these most difficult circumstances.

How can you be a good parent when you're on the edge or in the middle of an alienation situation? As a parent who's experiencing some symptoms of alienation you have to be even more careful, even more thoughtful. You have to go about becoming more than you ever expected of yourself.

The alienated parent has to be respectful, responsible, and reliable for their children's emotional well-being. Now that sounds nice but when you're facing some really tough situations and really difficult questions it becomes harder and harder to remain levelheaded— to respond the way you should *all* the time.

Every piece of parenting you do as an alienated parent should build, enhance, or improve your relationship with your child. We all know parenting, like every relationship, takes work so if you're at this stage you're having particular troubles— your child is being despondent or not interacting— whatever their behavior is, there are solutions. Go to the bookstore, refer to the list of books provided, go to the library, go to parenting groups. Talk about it with people. You're not alone.

1. Provide the court with a parenting plan.

2. Understand the nature of the problem and focus on what to do about it.

   Don't play the victim.

3. Be proactive in seeking education about what is happening to you and your child. You are your own best advocate.

4. Do not add to the problem. Find out how you can create a more positive situation. Do not make the things worse than they are already.

5. Journal, Journal, Journal! All key interaction with your ex partner and your child. Be accurate. This information may be admissible in court.

6. Be vigilant about your visitation. Always call or pick up your children, even if you know that the children won't be there.

7. Focus on your child and enjoy the time you have together.

8. Take the high road. Never involve your child in your legal proceedings. Never talked badly about the other parent to their children. Protect your child from any discourse at all times.

9. Never violate court orders. Pay child support on time and live within the law of your state.

10. Try to be rational and reasonable and exhibit that you have your child's best interest at heart.

You can prove your former spouse wrong with your actions; your words won't do it. No matter what the alienator parent may be saying about you, if your behavior always exudes love, support, and compassion the power of what they hear will be diluted by what they experience. Your actions will prove the alienator's words wrong. Always be careful what you put in writing, letters and emails.

If however you react badly, defensively, or chastise, then you may be making your child's worst fears come true. A child's biggest fear is that they are unwanted, unloved, that you don't love them as much as you once did as a result of the divorce or something that they're doing. An alienating parent will exploit any or all of these child fears. It's up to you to use your actions day-to-day, week in and week out to prove all the alienating accusations are wrong. This is of course easier to do if you're in some of the milder stages.

Because controlling the situation may be difficult, it might be that the only and most potent control is self-control. In order to access control we suggest you keep going to the anger exercises. Don't get involved in petty infighting. Don't react emotionally to your children's volatile emotions. You have to be in complete and total control of your life, your emotions, your thoughts, your feelings, and your environment when your children are around.

Compassion means to be understanding about your child's precarious situation. They're in a situation where they may be being bullied into thinking or believing a certain things about you. The more you retaliate or try to convince them not to believe a certain thing, the more dire and threatening the emotional situation gets.

It ratchets up the stress; it turns up the temperature of the uncertainty of their life. Things become even more precarious for them if you are constantly trying to un-brainwash the alienator's programming. You have to be very, very careful and how you choose to address the alienating accusations or insinuations. The best bet is to not address them directly at all but just to continue to prove in every way through your behavior, your actions that you love and you support your child.

Be prepared to demonstrate your compassion for your child's precarious and awkward position through your words and actions. Don't allow them to talk about the other parents' wishes or demands or insults. Just stop them if they start. Just carefully and politely change the subject as often as possible and keep doing it every single time until they get the picture. Your compassion towards their situation means not bickering, or gossiping by simply setting an example instead of teaching how you go about things.

Another way you show compassion is to avoid using the same manipulative tactics, avoid exacerbating or worsening their situation by constantly referring to it, investigating it, exploring it, and just always picking and poking at them about it. Your children should not be used as spies into the 'ex's' state of mind so that you can figure out how to make their lives worse.

You can demonstrate compassion for your child's precarious emotional situation by understanding how vulnerable they feel, how difficult the alienating parent may be making their lives and their relationship with you.

Oddly enough behaving 'AS IF' is an excellent way to demonstrate compassion. When you behave 'AS IF' nothing is wrong, 'AS IF' your relationship can withstand any of the storms it is weathering, 'AS IF' everything will turn out completely fine. That is demonstrating the kind of compassion that an alienated child needs.

Keep in mind that your child is between a rock and a hard place. The only way out is up. And you can be the motivation that pushes them up, up towards a higher way of thinking, a better way of dealing with the 'problems'. You can be the example that shows them how to live in a better way, in a more evolved, more emotionally mature, more human way of being.

The following is an is an excerpt and inventory from "The Good Karma Divorce" to help you access your underlying beliefs about what you think is right to tell your children. For every truth you plan to tell your children, I suggest you first ask yourself how it might damage them. Regardless of how sophisticated your children may sound (thanks to the media and their access to the Internet), your children are not emotionally developed enough to know how to process harmful truths.

Once you are clearer about your own underlying beliefs, your children can be protected not only from what you say, but what you don't say. Unspoken negativity can be just as potent. I have heard parents say, "I have never said a word against their father/mother." They don't have to; there are a thousand ways to transmit negative sentiments non-verbally. The movement of the eyes alone can convey more than one hundred separate and distinct emotions, opinions, and impressions.

Truth, while essential to the trust you create with your children, does not include topics that would malign their other parent or in any way hurt the child. You might say to me: "My wife cheated on me. Aren't my children supposed to know the truth? Are you asking me to tell them the truth, or are you asking me to lie to them so I don't hurt them?" If I asked you to list 20 things your spouse has done wrong, you may be right about most of them. The key question is: Is being right, or being honest, when it may do harm, more important than your child's happiness?

Being willing to do this exercise—and it is difficult—is one of the finest examples of heroic parenting I know:

- *Make a list of all the lies (even white lies) you have told your children about your breakup.*
- *Make a list of every time you exaggerated the bad behavior of your spouse to make yourself look better.*

- *Make a list of all your perceived truths that, if you communicated them to your children, might hurt them.*

Are you willing to set aside some of the more damaging elements of the truth for now in order to protect your children in their vulnerable state? Learning damaging things about a parent would be similar to the adult experience of being betrayed by a loved one or friend. It completely destabilizes your reality.

- *If you have more than one child, give each child some private attention every visiting time.*

- *Don't criticize your child's emotions; they are very real. Don't tell them they should "get over" something.*

- *Share with your children how you handled social difficulties when you were their age. Be honest about what you didn't handle well, and talk about how you see things differently now.*

- *Do not criticize, malign, or in any way speak poorly of your ex-spouse or spouse.*

- *Do not argue or fight with your former spouse in front of your children. If your former spouse insists on doing this bring a recorder and tell your spouse you want to record the sessions.*

- *Unfortunately, it is not easy to hide bad moods from your children. Because many children consider a divorce their fault, it follows that many children will naturally consider your bad mood their fault as well. It is important to explain to them that your mood is not based on anything they have done. If they have done something inappropriate and you overreact, explain to them that you may be overreacting because you are thinking about other things that don't have anything to do with them. The trick is to separate appropriate disappointment from agitated emotions that are a result of your divorce. It might be helpful to explain to them that you have had experiences before when you felt bad and have always gotten over them. This is a teachable moment to show them that bad feelings come and go.*

- *When your children are struggling with a situation, if applicable, it is a good idea to compliment them by telling them you know how difficult the situation was, and how well they handled it.*

Is Your Anger Affecting Your Children?

Make a list of things that will trigger your anger and cause you to act harshly or short- tempered with your children.

_____

_____

_____

_____

_____

_____

_____

_____

_____

_____

_____

_____

_____

_____

In addition to the skills Jill and I have learned from research and on our radio show *Family Matters*, here are some from "The Good Karma Divorce":

Each week take one of these things on your list and observe how it causes you to act or react with your children. Concentrate on one per week and see if you can modify your behavior. Ask your children, if they're old enough, to make a list of what they observe makes you angry or short-tempered. Tell them you will not be angry about anything they write on the list. Tell them that you are going to work on one of the things on their list per week.

Your child is not your therapist. Sharing your ongoing worries with your children may teach them chronic anxiety as a way of life. As an adult, you may no longer worry after the problem has been resolved, but as a child, long-term anxiety about a subject you have gotten over can make imprints in the soft clay that forms your child's emotional terrain.

If the grandparents have not chosen sides in an obvious and apparent way, and if they understand your commitment to non-malignment, they (together with other relatives) are an excellent source of emotional security. They may provide extra emotional reserves at the times you are feeling depleted. They also give a sense of family continuity.

Teachers and caregivers should be informed when parents are separating. Let them know who will be picking up the children from school, and whom to call in case of emergency. If you let them know what's going on, they can give your child extra attention and can apprise you of any problematic changes in your child's behavior. Teachers are often the first to notice a child is under stress.

Many schools have psychologists and social workers to help the children of divorce. Find out what resources are available. The social workers can help you get in touch with resources in your community. Most hospitals have sliding fee scales for children's therapy. Sometimes children feel quite lonely and could benefit from support groups, even if they are afraid to show their emotions.

Rituals restore or promote a sense of order and predictability. Restore old traditions as close as possible to their former structure, as they appear to be signposts of stability for the family. Create new rituals to reflect symbols of optimism for the newly configured family. Mealtime prayers are very comforting for young children and teenagers, while youngsters like bedtime prayers. The prayers do not have to be based on any organized religion, but might include expressions of gratitude.

We recommend that you avoid questioning your children about what occurred during, or how they felt about, time with the other parent. Often children are frightened that if they tell one parent they enjoyed their time with the other, the parent they are telling might love them less.

Sometimes children feel they are betraying one parent if they feel they have to say something negative to appease the questioning parent. This question of loyalty should not require children to have to improvise how to handle parents on every, or any, visitation. A child should not be required to keep two sets of books. They already may have a loyalty conflict imposed by the other parent, and you do not want to add to that.

- *Don't require your child to keep secrets from the other parent. Consider how difficult it is for you as an adult to keep a secret. Think about a child who fears that if he cannot keep a secret, he may lose the parent's love. Secrets can easily become terrifying requests.*
- *Give your child permission to say, "I don't want to talk about what happened at Mommy's house."*

Consistency

Above all parenting guides recommend consistency. At the core of the consistency issue is the idea that your child knows and learns what to expect from you under any circumstances. If you're a consistent parent your child knows that they can trust you and they'll learn to rely on you and lean on you on when it's appropriate and value your reliability had during hard times.

Consistency first and foremost is being consistent with your visitation. Consistency means consistent mealtimes, bedtime, and routines, the same punishment for the same infractions every single time. Consistency means doing what you'll say you'll do. Consistency means integrity— that your words match your actions and your actions match your words. By maintaining consistency you can actually wear down the attempted alienation simply by being a better version of you.

Consistency Exercise

The most important aspects of good parenting are communication, compassion, consistency, and control. We are now going to address your parenting consistency. You must be able to clearly articulate your boundaries, your rules, and the consequences of what happens when each child breaks these rules. If you don't know the answers to these questions how could your child know?

Your child should know that if they argue or backtalk in the car while you're driving somewhere what the consequences are. Your child should know that if they lie about where they're going, what the consequences will be. If you don't know if you can't write them down clearly...how can your child know what to expect?

If your child doesn't know what to expect from you there's going to be some fear in your relationship. There's no room for fear in an alienation situation.

So go ahead and write down your own parenting plan include and detail all your expectations and be clear about the consequences. What are the consequences of getting caught not doing homework? Or the consequences of getting caught lying to both parents? You should be able to note all the consequences for all infractions that you can think up.

Write down your own parenting plan that details mealtimes, bedtimes, rules, and expectations including the consequence of breaking the rules during visits.

Understand that you and your ex may have slightly different parenting styles and within a certain median that's okay. Although psychologists like routine, the children can still have the close enough to the same with an individual flavor. Your children will still be successful even if they go to bed an hour half an hour 45 minutes later or earlier....they'll still be fine if their diet makes some changes from one parent to another. As long as you're consistent they will know what to expect and consistently is what breeds results not rigidity. You can parent slightly different and in your own way without creating any problems for the other parent and vice versa.

Dealing with The Alienator

One of the biggest issues that alienated parents face is...the problem seems to be *somebody else*. It seems like if you could just make the 'ex' stop doing whatever they're doing everything would be okay but...it's not our job or our responsibility to 'change' others.

Of course the biggest drawback to the mentality that everything would be fine if only they would stop is...someone else is to blame. That means you can't do anything. This outlook infers that you can do nothing to alleviate the situation, that you are a victim. This is no way to move forward.

So how do you manage a relationship that's tense and fearful? How do you 'manage' someone who just seems to keep attacking and creating a crisis rather than trying to solve the problem?

The fact is when people are panicked; feel threatened...they become capable of terrifying things. So understand that you are handling an 'unreasonable,' 'fearful' person in crisis that you must deal with.

People do it all the time...that is; work with 'impossible' bosses, dictators, or even petty mad tyrants...when necessary. If the stakes are important enough we can call up our reserves of patience and sanity to do whatever needs to be done.

When we're dealing with someone who is aggressively haunting our sense of wellbeing the instinctive response is to counter-attack. You will be tempted to try and convince them why they are 'wrong', how many ways they're woefully wrong and how entirely justified and correct you are. The other person is dangerous to your sense of security; threatening your relationship with your children. So you have to be smarter, more wise, more evolved than them. This workbook is designed to prepare you to do just that by accessing ways to enhance your self-control.

For better or for worse it's not much different than what our parents and teachers told us when we were little dealing with bullies at school. They only have power over you that you 'give' them. It is possible to choose to rise above the wrestling in the mud. When people lose control lives are ruined, families get destroyed. Therefore it's solely up to you to keep your wits about you and learn to handle this 'other person' effectively.

9 Guidelines For Managing Impossible People

1. Don't Take it Personally

Your ex obviously has unresolved issues. They believe these 'issues' revolve around you. Yes, you'd like to get along and live in peace but they keep creating one problem after another for you and your children. The best way to approach the situation is for you get as much intellectual, emotional distance from the storm as possible. Accept that 'they' are unhappy and there is nothing you can (or should be doing about it). Even though they are 'taking it out on you' you are really not the source of their real pain.

The truth is if you can simply practice *imagining* watching their drama as if it was a bad TV show, or the story of a friend-of-a-friend, or as if it's the drama of a made for TV movie you can stay detached, keep yourself out of the muck. Not taking their behavior, their attacks, or their attempts to separate you from your children as 'personal' may sound like a tall order but it's true. They are fighting their own projected fears and worries. They are at war with their own issues. They are just attaching the 'problems' to you because you're a convenient target, an easy scapegoat for 'everything' that's wrong with their lives, for everything that's wrong with their relationships with their children.

To Act 'AS IF' is a powerful exercise like we did when we talked about parenting. Think, speak, and act 'AS IF' your ex is fighting with some imaginary fear, some scapegoat and not you. Imagine their threats and accusations aimed at some invisible phantom standing behind you. You'll be pleasantly surprised at what imagining this will do for your behavior. If you can just keep picturing that your ex is fighting against not you but against some 'unseen' menace it can change the way you think and feel. This is the whole point of the exercise—for you to 'feel better.' For you to be able to cut yourself out of the 'ex's' drama and see the situation for what it really is.

It's elementary Psychology 101 to recognize that their fight is not solely with you you'll find that you start behaving, thinking, and feeling less stressed about the whole thing. Because it is most important that you are in a healthy, whole state of mind for being a good parent to your child, for keeping your wits about you and not letting yourself get drawn into battles that aren't even really yours to fight.

2. Identify Their Fears

The next best way to deal with difficult or 'impossible' people is to 'walk a mile in their shoes'. Experts recommend considering what the 'difficult' person is afraid of, consider what fear is motivating their behavior. Relationship problems arise when people are motivated by different fears.

For example someone who values getting thing done quickly 'on time' may be afraid of missing a deadline. Someone who values accuracy fears what happens when things are done incorrectly.

Consider what fears may be driving your ex's alienating behavior.

_____
_____
_____
_____
_____
_____
_____
_____
_____
_____
_____
_____

Just being aware of another person's fears gives you the advantage in handling their difficult behavior. Stephen Covey says, "We see the world not as it is, but as we are."

3. Boundaries

The next expert tip for dealing with difficult people is boundaries. If you have to work with your enemy stay focused on whatever the task at hand is. If that's getting the time set for you to pick up the children—stick to that on the phone. Don't discuss anything else. Be business-like with your ex. We call it a wall of 'polite'. This tactic has the advantage of being impossible to criticize. Treat them with dignity and respect but get things switched over to an impersonal level. It's your job to emotionally distance yourself from your ex.

If they start to pick a fight, don't get into it with them. Refuse to engage in their battle. Instead, stay calm and level headed. Address the situation calmly if it must be addressed. But most such things don't even need a response. Most things the ex instigates, you must walk away from without engaging. Remember the question; 'Do I want to be 'right' or do I want to be sane?' Choose sane every time.

At this point in the relationship there is nothing you can say to their arguments that will change their minds or create peace so just don't go there.

Here are a few more don'ts in the boundaries department.

4. Don't start arguments.

5. Don't let them engage you in arguments.

6. Don't think you have to pretend to be 'friends' just yet (that may come later).

7. Don't pass comments on their life; who they are dating, their work, their friends…on anything.

8. Don't instigate- don't intentionally do things- like bring the children home late- just to stick it to them.

9. Don't brag or talk about your 'new' life of freedom. Keep things business-like and impersonal.

Alienation in the Courts

There is a difference between justified refusal of a child to visit and an alienated child. Some courts blur the distinction so it is essential to point out the difference. Children who have been abused or are ill may have justifications but there are not many other than those. Some courts think ordering the alienating parent to encourage visitation is good enough. The courts should send the message and include in the court orders that the alienating parent should *require* the child to go on visitation.

Some courts leave the decision about visitation up to the children. However this overly empowers children to disobey rules and authority which could adversely affect their future functioning. Therefore courts should not allow the children to decide about the visitation.

Some courts overly rely on supervised visitation. Supervised visitation sends the message to the child that the target parent is dangerous. But the targeted parent *should* go on the supervised visits if that is all they can get. The courts will see it as a negative if at parent doesn't do 'whatever it takes' to see their child.

Some courts believe that children should not be stressed out by conflicting opinions. Children need time with the alienated parent so they can develop the skills of balancing the facts in later life. The distorted thinking left intact could affect other areas of their lives.

Alienated parents should not modify the court orders on their own. You need either the other parents' permission in writing or a modification by court order. Judges take a very dim view of self-help when it comes to child support or visitation.

Many judges believe that in high conflict divorces there should be as little contact between the parties as possible. The courts must be educated that cutting back the alienated parents' *parenting time* is not an answer. The children will pay the price for the alienator's conduct.

Studies show that even children, who refuse to visit, still love the target parent. The courts can help the children with their loyalty dilemma by enforcing the parenting time. This in essence gets the children 'off the hook' with the alienating parent.

If the alienating parent is found to have given false testimony make sure you include that in your orders as well.   Ask the judge to impose monetary sanctions. Monetizing violations of visitation orders gets the violators' attention. Once reduced to a monetary fee or sanctions it is easier to find the violator in contempt. False allegations, once proven to be false should be penalized by the court.

Some courts believe that when children are older it is too late to repair the relationship with the targeted parent.   As long as I have jurisdiction I (Judge Michele) think it is never too late. If the child goes into adulthood and has severed an important relationship without attempts at resolution, usually through therapy, the value of future relationships might be diminished as well.

When A Spouse Remarries Or Has An Outside Relationship

For years I (Judge Michele) have observed explosive flare ups in a case when one spouse remarries or becomes emotionally involved with someone new. I must say you don't have to worry about judges understanding this flare up, they do. Here are some of the reasons to be very careful about this murky territory:

1. The new spouse feels their position is threatened by the former spouse and the new union is bonding over the perceived enemy.

2. Many alienating and even non alienating parents can be concerned for how their child is handling the new relationship, so they look legitimate in court. In fact I rarely see the child handling the new person well in a high conflict divorce. The child is in fact usually put into a further loyalty bind; one of the parents may still have unresolved feelings for the other parent. All of these flare ups also occur even when there it is just a boy or girl friend.

3. A new person may provide new resources, the old system becomes unbalanced because one parent has a new ally, a new competitor for the role of a parent, so there may be jealousy, envy of time spent with that parent.

The purpose of understanding this is that you need to be doubly ready to control your own reactions to the possibility of your former spouse's amped up emotions. Get ready to work on yourself...overtime.

Educate Yourself About Local County Rules

✓ Learn To Report A Violation of a Court Order

Find out what you should do if your alienator violates your shared parenting agreement or court order custody agreement. Some counties will ask that you call the police at the instance and file a complaint. Some counties may require you to file a 'request to show cause' or a 'motion to show cause' at your local county courthouse. You should research and know how violations of court orders should be handled in your home county *before* you have to do it.

✓ 12 Elements of A Request For Rule to Show Cause

This is the document you may need to file if your alienator violates your court ordered agreement. You should be able to download and print this as a document from your local county court's website. At the very least they will have hard copies available at the courthouse itself.

I (Judge Michele) am going to give you some general concepts about a rule to show cause or as it is sometimes called a Petition For Indirect Civil Contempt. This is not meant to be legal advice as there are many nuances depending on your facts and your location. But the more you know the better you will feel of availing yourself of this remedy.

If you have an attorney they will probably know what to do but when it comes to Parental Alienation and Visitation Interference, but too many target parents have run out of funds for sustained attorney's fees. Understanding how these petitions work will also help you prepare for what your attorney will need from you.

1. The purpose of this petition is to coerce and enforce compliance with a previous court order or Judgment or Decree for Divorce.

2. The petition must be signed under oath (verified) and filed in the original cause out of which the violation of the order arose.

3. State the exact time and date and portion of the original order which you feel has been violated.

4. State the exact time, a full description of the facts and circumstances and date in which the order was violated.

5. State that the violation was willful and that the violator had the means to comply with the order.

6. Go to court to get a date for presentation of your petition.

7. Give notice to the violator with a copy of your petition and a document called Notice of Motion letting them know the date of the hearing and what it is about (that will be stated in the petition).

8. Notice requirements are usually 5 to 7 days in advance of the hearing date.

9. Usually personal service (a sheriff or process server) is not required and regular U.S. mail to violators' last known address is enough.

10. If your visitation order is vague or 'reasonable visitation' it is not specific enough to find them in contempt of court.

11. The contemptor (respondent) does not have the right to court appointed counsel or a jury.

12. In some jurisdictions if a rule is entered against the violator they will have an opportunity to purge the contempt by allowing visitation during a period of probation.

You should learn how to file a 'Petition For Rule to Show Cause' or 'Request to Show Cause' at your local county courthouse. Find out from a local attorney whether you should file each incident at the time or whether you should keep records and demonstrate a 'pattern' of violations before you go to court. When you do go to court do not tell the judge (in the event your documents are incorrect) 'they told you to do it this way'. There is no 'they' that is responsible for your case unless it is your attorney.

Along with the Rule to Show Cause, you could also file a Petition for reconciliation therapy for your children or for family counseling. When orders are violated go to court as soon as possible, even if you have to end up going yourself. Don't delay.

Consider creating a 'visitation interference' diagram for the judge. Instead of voluminous pleadings you can demonstrate to the judge in five minutes a long record of violations and offenses in a chart. This can clearly show what couldn't be covered in five hours. The graphic you use should clearly show the number of visits canceled and demonstrate any trends for example increasing cancellations over months.

Use tables or bar graphs to indicate the frequency or type of violations that are recurring. Use another on the column for the dates of visits missed. Use different colors to indicate different categories; red for days your child refused to go, yellow for cancelations due to illness, purple for no excuse even offered, etc.

Use another method to indicate if you have written proof of the violation i.e. police report or email etc., use a *different* indicator for violations for which you have witnesses available.

Make a list of the "experts' alienating behaviors" from Part 1 and put a check mark in your table next to each of the behaviors your child has exhibited.

Make a graph showing the number of completed successful visits dropping drastically.

As an attachment to the chart always prepare a BRIEF summary of conversations that spread animosity to the children, friends and/or extended family.

Obtain frequent status and progress dates. Delay can be the enemy.

✓ Order of Protection

Another legal hurdle that many alienated parents confront is a restraining order or 'Order of Protection' being entered against them. Generally restraining orders and Orders of Protection allow the court to order someone to stay away from another person, from their home, from their workplace, from their school, and to stop contacting them and protect them from harassment of any kind or violence.

Victims can usually also ask the court that all contact with them by telephone, notes, mail, fax, e-mail, texts, are all prohibited. This system was designed to help protect victims from abuse and threats. This is why there is a very low burden of proof for restraining orders. This is when orders of Protection are used for proper purposes.

But too often this effective proceeding is used by the alienating parent to limit the target parent's relationship with their child. Protective Orders of a Court based on this kind of motivation may remove the accused target Parent from the home, bar the accused target parent from seeing his/her children, and give the Alienating Parent total physical custody of the children.

An alienating parent may be able to get a temporary order of protection, but issuance of a long-term protective order depends on a judge's assessment after a full hearing. The full hearing allows the accused target parent to present evidence, offer an explanation, and proceed with a lawyer's help, if necessary.

Getting representation may be very important at this point because if the alienator succeeds in getting an Order of Protection, your child may see you in a dangerous light. If the facts warrant it, you also will not want a supervised visit for the same reason. If the judge sees fit to give you only a supervised visit, even if only on a temporary basis, exercise that visitation.

Communicating With Officers of the Court

In a small town you may have to educate your attorney about parental alienation. Don't ask the attorney 'do you know what it is?' You may be surprised to find out that lawyers have egos. Just share with them what you have learned and researched. You should find out in the initial interview what they know.

Ask the judge to please keep an eye open toward alienating behavior as the case progresses. If you are pro se or even if you are the attorney you might prepare the judge for your return visit. You might say, "I hope this works your honor, but if it doesn't am sorry but I will have to come back. "

Judges like to believe that what they do works and it is the right decision. When their decision isn't working they often get exasperated with both parties. Make sure the judge is reminded of past violations (use visual aids as suggested earlier). When talking to most judges you should avoid the specific words 'Parental Alienation Syndrome' and stick to violations and missed visitations.

15 Tips For Presenting Yourself Well in Court

Court is a place where decorum, rules, propriety, and order still prevail. Here are a few suggestions that might be helpful.

1. Dress as if for a job interview.

2. Demonstrate self-control.

3. Don't interrupt.

4. Don't volunteer any information.

5. Don't speak unless spoken to.

6. No matter how angry you are, do not allow that anger to color your presentation to the judge. This is not the time to vent to the judge by giving them volumes of information.

7. Make attempts to learn what you can about what you are trying to do. Go on the internet or to law libraries.

8. Bring a pen and paper to write down what the judge says and the rulings.

9. Be prepared to write your own court order about what the judge says. Many court rooms have attorneys that might volunteer to help you but don't count on it.

10. Hand your papers including petition and notice and the last court order if any to the judge when your case is called.

11. If you are asking for family therapy, reconciliation therapy or therapy for your child come prepared with the names of appropriate therapists and their contact information.

12. You may want to bring a supportive friend who will keep you calm, report to you what has happened if you are too emotional, and take notes about what the judge says.

13. If you suspect that things are not going well for you in front of a certain judge you may want to bring your own court reporter.

14. If there is a finding of no abuse by a social service agency make sure you bring that document to court.

15. When you first get an indication of alienation do not wait to go to court, it has been my experience that it doesn't just go away. If there are either signs of

alienation or even findings by the court make sure you write this down in your court orders and Judgment. You may not have the same judge next time and you want to document the history of this issue being present in your case.

Be An Activist

I (Jill) have found that activism is such a large part of what alienated parents can do to help themselves heal. By taking an active role in advancing their cause, target parents participate in creating a long term solution that can prevent such a terrible thing from happening in other families. This may be small consolation for a severely (or fully) alienated parent who has lost all contact with their children. But it helps to share experiences with others and to try and search for solutions and education. Feeling less isolated is an added benefit. Activism puts us in touch with others who have shared many of our heartbreaking experiences and helps us feel a little bit less alone.

In my (Jill) support groups most newcomers feel a tremendous sense of relief to realize that they are not alone. Loneliness and keeping their pain a secret are hall marks of early stage alienation.

Many of you will be frightened by the advice that we will give you in this section of the workbook. If it is not your nature to want to be in the public eye, you will particularly shy away from this section. This is potentially one of the most important parts of your healing process. There is no one that is a better advocate for you and your child than you are going to become.

As we have indicated, there are many aspects to dealing with parental alienation and there are many different ways that you can be an effective advocate. We understand that there is a stigma attached to you not seeing your children. The general public will think that there is something wrong with you. Through education and awareness, you can explain parental alienation in a way that people who have not had experience with will be able to understand. This education and awareness can be achieved whether it is one on one or in a group. For example, you may want to start with a mental health professional you or your child are seeing, a school counselor or police department employee that must make decisions on custody and visitation interference calls. If you attend a place of worship, speak to your faith leader. Many places of worship now have divorce recovery classes. Get in touch with the facilitator of that group.

If you are comfortable speaking to large groups, check your local paper for Lions, Kiwanis, Rotary or other social, political, or educational groups that meet on a monthly basis. They are always looking for interesting speakers and timely topics. Attend events where you will be able to distribute brochures and other educational materials related to parental alienation. For example, health and wellness fairs are an excellent way to get the word out.

Another important element to implementing change is to contact your elected officials. Legislative change and judicial education are both integral parts of the keys to change in divorce culture. Legislators want to hear from you. They are there to act on constituent concerns and they cannot hear what you do not say. Call, make an appointment and explain to them the need for change in your state.

We have told you that you need a strong support system through your parental alienation journey. There are many parents who have no support at all and would benefit from an advocacy group meeting once a month. This will require finding a donated venue and free publicity to post your meeting time and date. My group in central Illinois is called the Parental Alienation Advocacy Forum. It is not a support group as we do not have a mental health professional involved; however there is a strong element of support in all of us being together and working to make changes that will protect children through divorce and beyond.

These are just a few of the ways that you can become active and redirect your energy in a positive and rewarding way. The possibilities for education and awareness are endless. Remember that if you are continuously looking in the rear view mirror, it will be difficult to see the road ahead.

Further Reading

A Kidnapped Mind: A Mother's Heartbreaking Story of Parental Alienation Syndrome by Pamela Richardson- www.akidnappedmind.com

Divorce Casualties: Protecting Your Children from Parental Alienation by Douglas Darnall.

The International Handbook of Parental Alienation Syndrome: Conceptual, Clinical And Legal Considerations by Richard A. Gardner, Richard Sauber, Demosthenes Lorandos (Editors)

Divorce Poison: Protecting the Parent/Child Bond from a Vindictive Ex by Dr Richard a. Warshak

Welcome Back Pluto (DVD) by Dr. Richard Warshak

Denied Access by David Chick

Children Held Hostage by Stanley S. Clawar

Adult Children of Parental Alienation Syndrome: Breaking The Ties That Bind by Dr. Amy Baker

The Look Of Love by Jill Egizii

The Good Karma Divorce by Judge Michele Lowrance

Children of Divorce: A Practical Guide for Parents, Therapists, Attorneys, and Judges by William Bernet, Don R. Ash

The Essentials of Parental Alienation by Robert A. Evans, Ph.D. and J. Michael Bone, Ph.D.

Parental Alienation (PA) & Parental Alienation Syndrome (PAS) by Dr. Jayne Major

A Family's Heartbreak: A Parent's Introduction to Parental Alienation by Mike Jeffries

Other Helpful Resources

Amy J.L. Baker PhD www.amyjlbaker.com

Joseph Goldberg -PA Medical/Legal Consultant- www.parentalalienation.ca

Dr. Reena Sommers- www.reenasommerassociates.mb.ca

Michael Bone, PhD- Parental Alienation Consulting-www.jmichaelbone.com

Dr. L. F. Lowenstein- Parental Alienation Consultant-www.parentalalienation.org.uk

Dean Tong- Forensic Consultant - www.abuse-excuse.com

Dr. Douglas Darnell- www.parentalalienation.org

Dr. Jayne Major- Breakthrough Parenting- www.breakthroughparenting.com

Dr. Richard A. Warshak- www.warshak.com

Dr. Kathleen Reay – www.kreaycounselling.com

Dr. Joan B. Kelley – www.ncmc-mdeiate.org/joan.html

Joshua Rose Foundation- www.joshuarosefoundation.webs.com

Rachel Foundation for Family Reintegration- www.rachelfoundation.org

A Family's Heartbreak- www.afamilysheartbreak.com

Parental Alienation Disorder- www.padsupport.wordpress.com

Equal Justice Foundation- www.ejfi.org/family/family-20.htm

The Lee P.A.S Foundation- www.theleepasfoundation.org

Dr. Richard Gardner- www.rgardner.com

Fathers are Forever- Radio Broadcast - Fridays 3:05-4:00 PST

KNRY 1240 AM - Santa Cruz, CA- Host: Steve Ashley- www.knry.com

ParentalAlienationAwarenessOrganization-www.parental-alienation-wareness.com

Shared Parenting Works- www.sharedparentingworks.org

Malicious Mom Syndrome- www.maliciousmom.blogspot.com

Parental Alienation Directory- www.padirectory.info

Split N Two- www.splitntwo.com

Made in the USA
Lexington, KY
26 April 2018